Biblical Inspiration and the Authority of Scripture

Biblical Inspiration and the Authority of Scripture

Carlos R. Bovell, editor

WIPF & STOCK · Eugene, Oregon

BIBLICAL INSPIRATION AND THE AUTHORITY OF SCRIPTURE

Copyright © 2015 Carlos R. Bovell. All rights reserved. Except for brief quotations in critical publications or reviews, no part of this book may be reproduced in any manner without prior written permission from the publisher. Write: Permissions. Wipf and Stock Publishers, 199 W. 8th Ave., Suite 3, Eugene, OR 97401.

Wipf & Stock
An Imprint of Wipf and Stock Publishers
199 W. 8th Ave., Suite 3
Eugene, OR 97401

www.wipfandstock.com

ISBN 13: 978-1-62564-241-7

Manufactured in the U.S.A.   06/24/2015

For students, young and old
May God give them grace to keep faith

Contents

Contributors | ix

Introduction | xi
—*Carlos R. Bovell*

Biblical Inspiration

All Scripture is Hermeneutically God-Breathed | 3
—*Carlos R. Bovell*

Responses

The Doctrine of Inspiration and the Dead Sea Scrolls | 27
—*George J. Brooke*

What is a Doctrine of Scriptural Inspiration *For*? | 32
—*Richard S. Briggs*

An "Inspired" Theory of Truth and a Pluralism Worthy of God | 44
—*Mark S. McLeod-Harrison*

The Authority of Scripture

The External Authority of Scripture | 59
—*Carlos R. Bovell*

The Internal Authority of Scripture | 90
—*Carlos R. Bovell*

CONTENTS

Responses

The Authority of Sacred Scriptures | 113
—*J. Harold Ellens*

A "Reflexive Trust" in the Authority of Scripture | 121
—*Holly Beers*

Jesus' Post-Resurrection Appearances in the Light of Full-Bodied Spirit Materializations | 128
—*Clint Tibbs*

Postscript

The Bible and Seminary Experience: We Need to Do More for Our Students | 153
—*Carlos R. Bovell*

Contributors

Holly Beers is Assistant Professor of Religious Studies at Westmont College. She is the author of *The Followers of Jesus as the 'Servant': Luke's Model from Isaiah for the Disciples in Luke-Acts*.

Carlos R. Bovell is an independent researcher. He is the author of *Inerrancy and the Spiritual Formation of Younger Evangelicals*, *By Good and Necessary Consequence: A Preliminary Genealogy of Biblicist Foundationalism*, and *Rehabilitating Inerrancy in a Culture of Fear*.

Richard S. Briggs is Lecturer in Old Testament and Director of Biblical Studies at Cranmer Hall in St John's College, Durham University, England. He is the author of *The Virtuous Reader* and *Reading the Bible Wisely*.

George J. Brooke is Rylands Professor of Biblical Criticism and Exegesis at the University of Manchester, England. He is the author of *Reading the Dead Sea Scrolls: Essays in Method*.

The Rev. Dr. J. Harold Ellens, University of Michigan, is retired. He is the author of *A Dangerous Report: Challenging Sermons for Advent and Easter*; *God's Radical Grace: Challenging Sermons for Ordinary Time(s)*; and *By Grace Alone: Forgiveness for Everyone, for Everything, for Evermore*.

Mark S. McLeod-Harrison is Professor of Philosophy at George Fox University. He is the author of *Make/Believing the World(s): Toward a Christian Ontological Pluralism* and *Apologizing for God*.

Clint Tibbs is Assistant Professor of Philosophy at Delta State University in Cleveland, Mississippi. He is the author of *Religious Experience of the Pneuma: Communication with the Spirit World in 1 Corinthians 12 and 14*.

Introduction

THE MATERIAL CONTAINED IN this book grew out of work done for a planned special issue of an evangelical journal on the inspiration of the Bible. For a number of reasons, I was delayed in getting the project off the ground. In the meantime, the journal itself underwent a phase of transition, including changes in editorial staff, which affected the decision to run a special issue on biblical inspiration in the first place. By God's providence, I believe, this new book format will be better positioned than the original journal issue to reach those believers who stand to benefit most from the discussion.

Over the years, I have developed a more definite idea of just what a new evangelical view of inspiration might look like. Yet it has also become clear that even believers who might be willing to shift their views about scripture may have a hard time doing so. I did not, therefore, want interested readers to feel isolated as they contemplated major shifts in their religious and spiritual thinking. So I approached a group of established scholars and asked if they might take time out of their busy schedules to offer responses to my proposals. This way, students and other readers can see what issues other researchers find to be important, issues that may differ from the concerns that readers themselves might raise, or from the concerns raised by their pastors and professors who come from an inerrantist context. Accordingly, I have arranged the book into two parts, a first that speaks to the Bible's inspiration and a second that ponders its authority. Each of these consists of a lead essay followed by three responses.

In my last edited volume, *Interdisciplinary Perspectives on the Authority of Scripture* (Pickwick Publications, 2011), I made sure that inerrantist authors were among the participants so that we could present inerrancy as still being a live option. My reason for doing so was to speak to a broad audience, including readers who, though committed to inerrancy themselves, were still genuinely interested in hearing what real problems inerrancy introduces to faith. Even so, it has been my view for some time now that the work that needs to be done in conservative evangelical bibliology cannot genuinely take place within the constraints of conservative evangelicalism. For that reason, many have found it much easier (and healthier) to exchange denominations altogether and join another tradition rather than remaining within evangelicalism and simply hoping that things will change. However, as soon as one leaves the social confines of American evangelicalism, there is no longer a reason to address inerrancy at all. On the other hand, if a believer stays within evangelicalism, it does not take long to realize that, because of the centrality evangelicalism affords to inerrancy, what is needed is not a clever modification here or there, but rather a reconceptualization of what faith itself is and how the Bible contributes to it.

In the current climate, such a suggestion may appear religiously and culturally unthinkable. Nevertheless, I sincerely believe that the future of evangelicalism will depend on a radical shift in its thinking on the inspiration and authority of scripture. If evangelical bibliology has any hope of emerging from its present ideological quagmire, evangelicals will need to imagine a rather different Bible than the one they are used to working with. The obstacles that impede such a change are more cultural than doctrinal. This came to my attention while taking classes in apologetics first at Liberty Theological Seminary and later at Westminster Theological Seminary, two conservative, inerrantist institutions. It did not take long to realize that regardless of whether one defends the faith evidentially (Liberty) or presuppositionally (Westminster), the way inerrantists go about proclaiming and defending orthodox Christian faith is profoundly out of touch with what students and scholars experience when studying both the Bible and church history in an objective or non-defensive mode.

Upon making this initial observation, I felt deeply obliged to try to *help* evangelical students. In many American evangelical schools and churches, inerrancy is still being taught as a watershed issue for faith, in spite of the difficulties raised by insisting upon it as a designation for the kind of scriptures God gave us. There are many young believers who will find this out in due time and will be forced to grapple with how to remain members of an evangelical community while unable to assent to the doctrine this community has chosen as its cultural signifier. Who will be there to help them sort through these issues? To whom can they turn for support as they struggle to hold on to faith and remain with their faith community even as they relinquish the doctrine of inerrancy?

Introduction

With this book, I seek to move beyond simply articulating why changes are immediately in order. In prior works, I tried to demonstrate the problems inerrancy raises for students and how it might be rehabilitated for them. In this book, by contrast, I try to describe what a new view of inspiration and authority can look like. Though I have moved further away from the inerrantist position in the intervening time, I still consider inerrantist (and post-inerrantist) readers to be my main conversation partners in this new book. I want to work with you to reestablish that deep trust we all have in scripture on a better foundation; rather than connecting scripture's redemptive trustworthiness to its historical-critical data, I wish to ground it in the vibrant power of God.

Although theology must play a central role in constructing a new doctrine of biblical inspiration and authority, it would be perilous for churches to forego engagement and outsource the task and leave it for theologians alone. Likewise, theologians should not be the ones to *begin* the conversation, at least not without carefully listening to what is happening in other disciplines. Therefore, rather than invite theologians to the discussion prematurely, I thought it would be more fruitful to have researchers in other fields ask some preliminary questions first. Only then might we present something substantial for the theologians to evaluate, and at such a stage assess the work.

I would like to acknowledge the staff at Wipf and Stock for all they have done in helping me connect with evangelical students and readers; the contributors for taking an interest in my work and devoting time to offering responses; Reverend Harald Peeders, a good friend and constant encouragement; my wife, still smiling when we roll up our sleeves to make those carimañolas; and my kids: it is for the sake of the spiritual formation of future students like them that I have not walked away from the inerrantist roundtable just yet.

Biblical Inspiration

All Scripture Is Hermeneutically God-Breathed

Carlos R. Bovell

IN RESPONSE TO A 1983 article by James Dunn, Roger Nicole found occasion to say that "the kind of book God wanted the Bible to be is the kind of book he declares it to be in verses like the pillar passages and many others . . . to wit, God-breathed, his word, of indefectible authority, clothed with God's own truthfulness."[1] Nicole seeks to take the "God-breathed" passage of 2 Tim 3 (along with others) and enumerate a list of properties that Scripture must possess on account of its participation in "God's own truthfulness."[2] In this essay, I present a different approach, one prompted by my reading of 2 Tim 3:16–17 in light of the Gospel of John. I suggest that inspiration is more fruitfully understood as follows: *because* the Scriptures possess the vitality of God, they will always be hermeneutically *useable* by believers for the various purposes set out in 2 Tim 3:16–17. More specifically, the Scriptures are always ready *to be made alive* because they have been specially prepared by God's Spirit to be filled with life by the Spirit whenever believers resort to them for the purposes listed in 2 Tim 3:16–17. In other words, the abiding "sense" of 2 Tim 3:16 is that "All Scripture is *hermeneutically* God-breathed."

1. Synopsis of the proposal

To make this work, I place a great deal of emphasis on the Johannine conception that the disciples were unable to find life in Scripture until they were given the Spirit by Jesus. According to Richard Bauckham, the Gospel of

---

1. Roger Nicole, "Inspiration and Authority of Scripture I," *Chm* 97 (1983): 206–207.

2. I critique the Chicago Statement on Biblical Inerrancy on these same points in *Rehabilitating Inerrancy in a Culture of Fear* (Eugene, OR: Wipf and Stock, 2012).

John adapts an existing Jewish tradition that held that "the Messiah will be a man who will not be known to be the Messiah until God reveals him to be [so]."[3] The fourth Gospel presents a scenario wherein those who walked with Jesus would have been unable to read Scripture in light of Jesus' life and crucifixion until after God revealed to them *that he was the Christ*. In other words, irrespective of any prior messianic readings they had of the Jewish Scriptures of the time, these could not have been readings they would have thought to apply to Jesus *during his lifetime*.[4] It was only *after* God had revealed Jesus as messiah—a post-resurrection experience indicated in John's Gospel by Jesus' literally breathing the Spirit into them—that the disciples, in turn, "breathed life" into Scripture in order to find life in its words.

Indeed, once it was revealed to them that Jesus was the messiah (that is, after the resurrection), they went back and tried to show that *his entire life* was messianic. This involved what Barnabas Lindars calls the "double process" of both proving from Scripture that Jesus' ministry was messianic and tweaking the idea of *what it meant to be messianic* so that they could convincingly align Scripture with Jesus' actual life.[5] Or as Klyne Snodgrass puts it, "They did not find texts and then find Jesus. They found Jesus and then saw how the Scriptures fit with him."[6] According to A. T. Hanson, the disciples were deliberately asking: "What light does this passage throw on the nature, career, and present significance of Jesus Christ?"[7] If these historical-critical findings are correct, the evangelical position of restricting inspiration to the texts and their authors may need to be rethought.

Philosopher and NT scholar Ben Meyer defines "ascription" as a hermeneutical activity wherein a reader assigns meaning to a text that "from the start is considered largely or at least partly indeterminate and open to

---

3. Richard Bauckham, "Messianism according to the Gospel of John," in *Challenging Perspectives on the Gospel of John*, ed. J. Lierman (Tübingen: Mohr Siebeck, 2006), 61.

4. Compare Martyn J. Selman, "Messianic Mysteries," in *The Lord's Anointed: Interpretation of Old Testament Messianic Texts*, ed. P. Satterthwaite, R. Hess, and G. Wenham (Grand Rapids: Baker, 1995), 300–302.

5. Barnabas Lindars, *New Testament Apologetic: The Doctrinal Significance of the Old Testament Quotations* (Philadelphia: Westminster, 1961), 186.

6. Klyne Snodgrass, "The Use of the Old Testament in the New," in *The Right Doctrine from the Wrong Texts? Essays on the Use of the Old Testament in the New*, ed. G. K. Beale (Grand Rapids: Baker, 1994), 39.

7. Anthony Tyrell Hanson, *The New Testament Interpretation of Scripture* (London: SPCK, 1980), 14.

determination."[8] If the history of biblical interpretation is any indication, the indeterminacy of biblical texts is not a matter that only the earliest Christians had to reckon with; churches throughout history also had to grapple with the same issue, and this includes twenty-first-century evangelicals. Just as the Old Testament remained "open to determination" by the disciples until Jesus was revealed to them as messiah (i.e., post-resurrection—when Jesus breathed the Holy Spirit into them), the Scriptures today remain open to determination by communities of believers that have also been filled with the same Holy Spirit. Evangelicals call this facet of the Spirit's work "illumination." I would like to consider whether this might be more fruitfully construed as "inspiration." My concern is with trying to better account for the role the Holy Spirit plays in the composition, transmission, and reception of Scripture by expanding the evangelical notion of biblical inspiration to encompass more than just the authors and the texts. I am seeking to integrate the formative and communicative aspects of Scripture into a more comprehensive doctrine of inspiration.

Admittedly, evangelicals have not generally been open to this idea. At least three factors contribute to their reluctance:

1. Evangelicals begin with a "prophecy model" for their picture of biblical inspiration and work outwards theologically from there.[9]
2. Evangelicals are particularly concerned with retaining the significance of the divine origin of Scripture, which encourages them to singularly focus on what it means for Scripture to be "God-breathed" (*theopneustos*).[10]
3. Evangelicals are orthodoxy-conscious and have adopted a biblicist-foundationalist approach to establishing and maintaining orthodoxy.

As a result, evangelicals are culturally predisposed to develop and augment the "good and necessary"[11] consequences of their conception of Scripture

---

8. Ben Meyer, "A Tricky Business: Ascribing New Meaning to Old Texts," *Greg* 71 (1990): 747.

9. Following Old Princeton's lead, evangelicals seek to stay as close as they can to dictation (a theory that fell into disrepute during the nineteenth century) while at the same time attempting to steer clear of its weaknesses.

10. For example, Loraine Boettner (*The Inspiration of the Scriptures* [Grand Rapids: Eerdmans, 1937], 33–34) claims: "There is no other term in the Greek language which would have asserted more emphatically the Divine origin of the product."

11. A phrase appearing in the Westminster Confession of Faith, 1.6. For the critique I

as prophetic and God-breathed (that it is verbally and plenarily inspired, that it is inerrant, etc.).

In many ways, the evangelical view of Scripture underlies all of evangelical theology, which includes its schemes of salvation.[12] For evangelicals, then, much rides on a correct view of the inspiration and authority of the Bible, and for some believers, this includes their salvation. The present chapter is intended as a road map to what an alternate picture of inspiration might look like. Its ideas are exploratory and preliminary, reflecting on issues in biblical theology, biblical studies, and philosophy.

2. Scripture and humans as in-spired

I begin by drawing attention to how Scripture and human beings are both "God-breathed." According to Goodrick, "Every Scripture, because it is theopneustic, is profitable" is how Origen read 2 Tim 3:16. After showing that the grammatical emphasis of verses 16 and 17 is on the word "profitable" (*ōphelimos*) and not "God-breathed" (*theopneustos*), Goodrick proposes the following translation: "For Scripture, alive as it is with the vitality of God himself, is valuable for indoctrinating people, for rebuking people who should know better, for correcting people who do not, for guiding people, so that God's man can be completely equipped for every good work."[13] The point of this pericope in 2 Tim, according to Goodrick, is that *because* God's breath of life somehow indwells the Scriptures, they can effectively be used for the accomplishing of God's purposes for the church, ultimately placing believers in a position to do God's will.[14] Thus, the Scriptures are filled with God's vitality and that is why they can come alive, that is why they *do* what they *do* in the service of God's people—in a word, that is how they are *ōphelimos* ("useful" or "profitable").

---

have in mind, see Bovell, *By Good and Necessary Consequence: A Preliminary Genealogy of Biblicist Foundationalism* (Eugene, OR: Wipf and Stock, 2009).

12. Another concern is that if evangelicals were to adopt non-evangelical approaches to inspiration, they would be calling into question their religio-cultural identity by undermining evangelical theological distinctions.

13. E. Goodrick, "Let's Put 2 Timothy 3:16 Back in the Bible," *JETS* 25 (1982): 486. Goodrick gives Origen's rendering of 2 Tim 3:16 in n10 on this same page.

14. Compare John P. Meier, "The Inspiration of Scripture: But What Counts as Scripture? (2 Tim 1:1–14; 3:14–17; cf. 1 Tim 5:18)," *Mid-Stream* 38 (1999): 75. Meier stresses that ministers in particular have been placed in this position.

Compare this with the image presented in Gen 2 where the first human being is portrayed as coming to life by virtue of God's breathing his spirit or wind into him. Once they possess God's vitality, humans are then positioned to come alive and do what God expects of them. In Gen 6:3, the Lord God says that he will not have his spirit live within human beings forever but rather will begin limiting their lifespan to one hundred and twenty years. Once again, the presumption is that with God's spirit, human beings are able to do what they do, but without it, they are not able to do anything at all.

In Ezek 37, Ezekiel is asked to prophesy to dead bones with the intent of making them come alive. After prophesying to the bones, he is told to prophesy to the breath since, without God's breath, they will not be able to come alive. The Lord then says to Israel, "I will give my breath into you and you shall live." In Job 27:3 there is a similar poetic parallel. "As long as I have life within me" is paired with "the breath of God in my nostrils." Job 33:4 gives another example of the same sequence: "The Spirit of God has made me, the breath of the Almighty gives me life." In sum, without God's "vitality"—to use Goodrick's word—human beings are unable to do what they were intended to do. Without God's breath, they cannot do anything at all.

For present purposes, the observation to make is that both human beings and the Scriptures are portrayed as God-breathed, with the implication that by virtue of possessing God's spirit—by virtue of God's creative act of breathing life into them—the two respective entities, humans and Scripture, are thought to be in possession of God's very "life," his "vitality."

3. "Eternal" life attributed to the Spirit, not Scripture

A dominant literary motif in John's Gospel is that of God giving life to Jesus' followers in a way that differs from the way he gives life to the rest of his creatures. The "life" that his people (i.e., believers in Jesus) possess is thought to be something more than the common life every human being experiences via the breath of God that they, too, presumably possess. In other words, Jesus' followers do not merely have life (God's breath), but they have it more abundantly as it were—life beyond life.

Throughout John's Gospel is expressed the belief that the followers of Jesus possess God's Spirit in a special way. John 3:8, for example, depicts Jesus as explaining this to Nicodemus: "The wind blows where it chooses," Jesus says, "and you hear the sound of it, but you do not know where it comes from or where it goes. So it is with everyone who is born of the Spirit." The Johannine view is that after Jesus' resurrection, his followers receive peculiar religious privileges and enhanced spiritual abilities. Both in this pericope and throughout the Gospel, the author develops variations of this theme. In John 3:14–15 for instance, the evangelist portrays Jesus as saying that the Son of Man must be "lifted up" so that "whoever believes in him may have eternal life." In John 3:16, it is written: "For God so loved the world that he gave his only Son, so that everyone who believes in him may not perish but may have eternal life." Here again is a reference to "eternal life," a special dispensation of God's Spirit that, according to the fourth Gospel, sets believers apart from ordinary human beings. John 3 closes with vv. 34–36: "He whom God has sent speaks the words of God, for he gives the Spirit without measure. The Father loves the Son and has placed all things in his hands. Whoever believes in the Son has eternal life; whoever disobeys the Son will not see life, but must endure God's wrath."

These summative remarks at the end of chapter 3 provide comment on a dispute between John the Baptist's disciples and an unnamed Jew. I posit that they, and each of the evangelist's subsequent parenthetical remarks, are to be read in light of what we find at the end of chapter 2: "But he was speaking of the temple of his body. After he was raised from the dead, his disciples remembered that he had said this; and they believed the Scripture and the word that Jesus had spoken." These words give a pneumatological basis for each of the passages of commentary that follow within the fourth gospel. Readers are told *how* the author came to a position in which he could see what he sees *in Scripture generally* and *in Jesus' words specifically*. He (and believers like him) have a spiritual capacity to see and understand what others who lack that capacity are not able to see or understand. My contention is that precisely those two facets of spiritual activity are what properly constitute biblical inspiration. The first is *the words of Scripture*, in whatever form they take throughout the long process of their growth, transmission, and reception. The second is *the hermeneutical matrix provided for Scripture by readers of Scripture*—but not just *any* readers: only readers *who possess the Spirit*, the Spirit of Life that would be given to them *after* Christ has been "glorified."

In *History and Theology in the Fourth Gospel*, James L. Martyn lists seven affirmations regarding what Jews of the time believed about Moses (both explicitly and implicitly). According to Martyn, one of the implicit affirmations of the Jews who are mentioned in the Gospel of John is that

> True confidence of *gaining life* by exegetical activity seems to rest on a) a belief that in order to receive the Law, Moses ascended to God on Sinai; in his ascent he was granted a vision of heavenly things; b) a conviction that by placing one's hope in Moses—by in fact believing in him, that is by truly hearing the voice of Moses, the shepherd whom God commissioned for Israel—one may oneself be granted heavenly visions.[15]

Martyn regards his seven affirmations as being "representative of the very life nerve of Judaism" and contrasts them with what the members of the Johannine community affirmed. In Martyn's reading of John, "the issue is not to be defined as an argument about an ancient text. It is not a midrashic issue." Both the Jews mentioned in John's gospel and the disciples of Jesus would view the Scriptures as able to impart life, but they disagreed as to how. The former argued that it came about through believing and attending to Moses. The latter argued that, on the contrary, "one may see a typological relationship only after having been grasped by God . . . never before being so grasped."[16] Interestingly, Martyn further observes that: "*It is, therefore, precisely the Paraclete who creates the two-level drama*"; the "two-level drama" is one of the features that distinguishes John from the synoptics.[17]

The ancient, cosmic dualism that viewed creation as compositionally divided into two distinct realms—the heavenly and the human ("In the beginning God created the heavens and the earth"[18])—has now been eschatologically ruptured by the appearing of the chief heavenly, as it were, making his home among humans, not in a temple as one might expect, but in and among the people personally, in Spirit and truth. Moreover, by virtue of Jesus' personally giving the Spirit to his disciples, the enduring presence of the divine (compare John 14:4: "remain in me and I also remain in you") via the Spirit inaugurates the next phase of redemptive history, where the human realm, although still very much human, can become a place in which the chief heavenly will always be immediately present to humans for visions and knowledge, but most importantly, for *salvation*. As Marie Isaacs observes, "For both John and Paul *pneuma* is therefore associated with the

---

15. James Louis Martyn, *History and Theology in the Fourth Gospel* (3d ed.; Louisville, KY: Westminster John Knox, 2003), 102, emphasis added.
16. Ibid., 123.
17. Ibid., 140.
18. And now interestingly in John 1:1: "In the beginning was the Word . . ."

dawning of the Messianic Age . . . it is *pneuma hagion* or *pneuma theou* breaking into human history in a unique and final way."[19]

In John 6:63, the author of John's Gospel depicts Jesus as belaboring this point, not to "the Jews" as one might expect, but to *his own disciples*. He states that their understanding of his words comes only by means of the life that is imparted by the Spirit. In v. 60, the disciples are portrayed as musing among themselves, "This teaching is difficult; who can accept it?" In v. 63, we find an interesting Johannine interpretation of the problem, which is presented, of course, as coming from the mouth of Jesus himself: "It is the spirit that gives life; the flesh is useless. The words that I have spoken to you are spirit and life."

In a similar way, John 5:19 describes Jesus as doing exactly what the Father does. Verse 21 of this chapter emphasizes that what the Father does is "raise the dead and give them life." This is something the Son will also do. Verse 24 gives the summary: "Very truly, I tell you, anyone who hears my word and believes him who sent me has eternal life." Verse 26 offers the eschatological interpretation of the pericope that I want to appropriate for biblical inspiration: there is a connection between being imbued with God's life and possessing his vitality that allows believers to make the Scriptures come alive, by *hermeneutically* breathing life into them, by, in a word, "in-spiring" them.

John has Jesus explain: "For just as the Father has life in himself, so he has granted the Son also to have life in himself." Several commentators have been quick to point out that what follows in John 5 seems to emphasize Jesus' authority for judgment. However, John depicts Jesus as explaining that the Scriptures, when left to themselves, do not grant eternal life. It is only to the extent that they are read within the hermeneutical framework provided for *by the Spirit* that "in them" one can have eternal life. The Scriptures give life because they testify to Jesus. Martyn describes Jesus' approach to Scripture in the fourth Gospel as follows: "John allows Jesus paradoxically to employ a form of midrashic discussion in order to terminate all midrashic discussion! Far from being predicated on certain exegetical patterns . . . faith has only one essential presupposition: the presence of Jesus and his self-authenticating word."[20]

---

19. Marie E. Isaacs, *The Concept of Spirit: A Study of Pneuma in Hellenistic Judaism and Its Bearing on the New Testament* (London: Heythrop College, 1976), 100.

20. Martyn, *History and Theology*, 123.

It has been noted by Hanson and others that the Jesus of John's Gospel is serving as "the mouthpiece for John's christology."[21] According to C. H. Dodd, John's Gospel is reminiscent of Greek philosophy in the way that it capitalizes on the genre of dialogue to get across its main points.[22] What I seek to add to this construct is that the Jesus of the Gospel of John offers us a conception of the Spirit that seems to have far-reaching implications for an evangelical doctrine of Scripture.

To help see this, consider how Hanson, who is not an evangelical, interprets the pastoral motivations for writing the Johannine Gospel in the first place:

> We may imagine him saying: If you find the cross and human limitations of Jesus a stumbling block, this is the way to think of him. This is the Christ of our post-resurrection experience. If it helps you in order to receive and maintain that experience to think of the incarnate Lord as I have depicted him, well and good. He may not indeed have been exactly like that, but imagining him this way is an aid to Christian devotion and a fence against false christologies.[23]

In an analogous way, I suggest that through the evangelist's conception of God's Spirit as breaking into history and perpetuating the presence of Jesus among believing communities, John also understands the Spirit to be breaking into Scripture through a believing hermeneutic with the result that Spirit-filled believers make the Scriptures come alive so that the Scriptures possess words of eternal life.

4. The Holy Spirit in-spiring believers and Scripture

Hanson observes that it is Scripture working in concert with the Spirit that makes John's christology possible. "The two indeed go together," writes

---

21. Anthony Tyrrell Hanson, *The Prophetic Gospel: A Study of John and the Old Testament* (Edinburgh: T & T Clark, 1991), 332.

22. See C. H. Dodd, "Dialogue Form in the Gospels," *BJRL* 37 (1954): 54–67.

23. Hanson, *Prophetic Gospel*, 332. Compare Georg Strecker (*Theology of the New Testament* [trans. M. Eugene Boring; Louisville, Ky.: Westminster John Knox, 2000], 460–461): "The fact of the matter is that the extensive absence of allusion to Synoptic materials in the Johannine letters permits the inference that most of the Johannine circle was unaware of the Gospel literature, *or at least did not consider it essentially important* [emphasis added]. The fourth evangelist wanted . . . by making limited use of fragments of Synoptic tradition, to write *the* Gospel of the Johannine circle."

Hanson. " . . . John no doubt believed that his claims for the function of the Paraclete after the resurrection, which include no doubt the teaching of his own advanced christology, were justified by what he had read in Scripture about the part the Spirit was to play in the messianic age."[24] I suggest that, in a similar way, the Spirit and Scripture come together in the evangelist's post-resurrection experience of Jesus *to make Scripture come alive*, which thereby makes it fit for redemptive, hermeneutical appropriation by God's people. The picture is one of Spirit-filled followers of Jesus hermeneutically interacting with Spirit-filled words of life.

At the beginning of the fourth Gospel, John the Baptist sees the Spirit "descending from heaven like a dove" and "remaining" on Jesus. In fact, in John's Gospel, this is precisely how John the Baptist would understand that Jesus "baptizes with the Holy Spirit." Yet as D. Moody Smith observes, in the fourth Gospel, Jesus is never baptized by John the Baptist.[25] It is clearly Jesus' Spirit-baptism that interests the evangelist, along with the fact that his disciples subsequently *received* the Spirit. The fourth Gospel places a great deal of emphasis on the fact that the Spirit that Jesus was baptized with is the same Spirit that Jesus *baptizes with*. My suggestion is that an overlooked role that Spirit-baptism plays for believers in the fourth Gospel involves their acquisition of a new hermeneutical capacity to bring life to Scripture in their post-resurrection interaction with it.

The picture that I have in mind is one where the Spirit in each of us "reaches out" to the Spirit in Scripture, making it come alive. I see a helpful analogy with prayer. In Rom 7, the apostle Paul explains that believers do not know how to pray as they ought.[26] To compensate for this, the Spirit intercedes for believers, which is what enables the meditative, human-divine connection. I suggest that scriptural inspiration works much the same way. The Spirit intercedes for believers, opening up the lines of communication between the Spirit that is in Scripture and the Spirit that is in believers. This is the mechanism by which the Bible is "in-spired." All of this is the work of the same Spirit. Both Scripture and human beings are each made alive by being separately infused with God's Spirit, but they are also *coordinately*

---

24. Hanson, *Prophetic Gospel*, 343.

25. D. Moody Smith, *The Theology of the Gospel of John* (New York: Cambridge University Press, 1995), 23.

26. Rom 7:26–27: "the Spirit too comes to the aid of our weakness . . . the one who searches hearts knows what is the intention of the Spirit, because it intercedes for the holy ones according to God's will."

enlivened in relation to one another by virtue of what I propose to call "biblical inspiration."

When M. Turner declares that "[i]t is not possible to identify, from Jesus' experience of the new age, covenant and kingdom by the Spirit, an archetypal element which was later shared by Christians,"[27] he is cautioning against reading too much into Jesus' baptism for insight into what believers can expect to experience when they receive the Spirit at their baptism.[28] In the case of John's Gospel, however, perhaps we are being encouraged to do exactly that. In Levison's study of how the phrase "filled with the Spirit" (and similar locutions) was understood in antiquity, he begins his treatment of the fourth Gospel with the same observation that I made above. Levison writes, "In the Fourth Gospel, the spirit may be the locus of wisdom, but not from birth. The spirit brings knowledge, but not until re-creation . . . The spirit brings truth, but only *after* Jesus is left to die on the cross. It brings instruction, but only *after* the resurrection."[29] Levison goes on to remark that many of the evangelist's ideas on the spirit are "by no means novel," but he also observes that "[w]hat is new is the certainty with which John locates the presence of the spirit at a point beyond the crucifixion."[30]

In Levison's view, there is an underappreciated, visceral description of the disciples receiving the Spirit from Jesus in John 22:22. He observes, "[T]he disciples, who once were void of the spirit, are now filled with the life-giving spirit-breath of Jesus himself."[31] Levison finds the *manner* in which the disciples receive the Spirit to be particularly striking. He draws attention to the fact that the disciples' Spirit-baptism is "preceded by an isolated and distinctive act: 'he breathed in them.'"[32] According to Levison, "The verb John selects to present us with this reality is *enephysēsen*, precisely the verb that is used in the Greek version of Gen 2:7: 'then the Lord God formed *adam* from the dust of the ground, and breathed into (*enephysēsen*) his nostrils the breath of life; and *adam* became a living being.'"[33] Although

---

27. M. M. B. Turner, "The Concept of Receiving the Spirit in John's Gospel," *VE* 10 (1977): 26 n17.

28. The early church would not typically have separated Spirit baptism from water baptism (as contemporary Evangelicalism tends to do). See G. W. H. Lampe, *The Seal of the Spirit* (2d ed.; London: SPCK, 1967), 45.

29. John Levison, *Filled with the Spirit* (Grand Rapids: Eerdmans, 2009), 366.

30. Ibid., 381.

31. Ibid., 379.

32. Ibid., 368.

33. Ibid., 369.

the effect of receiving the Spirit involves many complicated aspects of believers' spiritual development (e.g., the new birth), the point that is relevant for us here is succinctly expressed by Wyckoff: "Without the Holy Spirit, Scripture is a dead letter, but when he uses it to reveal God and his redemption in and through Jesus Christ, it is the living Word of God."[34] The Holy Spirit acts as "the angel of the book," as it were, functionally positioned within both the book and the book's readers to inerrantly mediate divinely authorized meanings.[35] Observations like these are often included in evangelical doctrines of illumination, but perhaps these more properly belong to a doctrine of biblical inspiration.[36]

5. The evangelical doctrine of inspiration

In his textbook *Christian Theology* for example, Millard Erickson champions Old Princeton's theological method and argues that by following the "teachings" of Scripture, believers will find that the Bible is *verbally* inspired, which is to say that the choice of words found in Scripture has been inspired by the Holy Spirit.[37] "By creating the thought and stimulating the

---

34. John W. Wyckoff, *Pneuma and Logos: The Role of the Spirit in Biblical Hermeneutics* (Eugene, OR: Wipf and Stock, 2010), 127.

35. See Stephen R. L. Clark, *The Mysteries of Religion: An Introduction to Philosophy through Religion* (New York: Basil Blackwell, 1986), 64–69. Clark suggests this is a weight that "a divine work of art" is surely able to bear.

36. Compare Mark Zia, *What Are They Saying about Biblical Inspiration?* (Mahwah, NJ: Paulist, 2011), 83: "Yet one renders this objective dimension of inspiration deficient if, in accepting its validity, one at the same time rejects the subjective dimensions of the Spirit's illuminative and ongoing transformative power within the life of the believer.... it is possible to affirm both the traditional Catholic and classical Protestant perspectives of biblical inspiration according to its objective and subjective dimensions." The Catechism of the Catholic Church explains: "But since Sacred Scripture is inspired, there is another and no less important principle of correct interpretation, without which Scripture would remain a dead letter. 'Sacred Scripture must be read and interpreted in the light of the same Spirit by whom it was written.'" See "The Catechism of the Catholic Church," n.p. [cited 4 May 2012]. Online: <http://www.vatican.va/archive/ccc_css/archive/catechism/p1s1c2a3.htm>. I am interested in finding a way to include this under "inspiration." The Catechism, for its part, claims both the authors and the books are divinely inspired, but I would like to see more made of the fact that *believers for whom the Scriptures are written* are also inspired.

37. See Millard Erickson, *Christian Theology* (2d ed.; Grand Rapids: Baker, 1998), 239. Erickson interacts a little with Dewey Beegle's preference for the "phenomena" of Scripture but claims in the end that both the teachings and the phenomena can be called upon to support the theory of verbal inspiration. I criticize the Old Princeton procedure

understanding of the Scripture writer, the Spirit will lead him in effect to use one particular word rather than any other."[38] Erickson goes on to outline what evangelical theologians call the doctrine of "plenary" inspiration, the idea that every Scripture is equally inspired: "The fact that we might be unable to identify the quality of inspiration within a particular passage should not alter our interpretation of that passage. We must not regard it as less authoritative."[39] The locus of biblical inspiration, then, is traditionally confined by evangelicals only to the authors and, in a derivative sense (so Erickson), the biblical texts themselves. I suggest that as the emerging generation of evangelical students mature in their studies, the traditional doctrine will prove less fruitful.

At least four main areas of investigation cumulatively support the idea of extending biblical inspiration beyond the locus of the authors and their writings: 1) what surprisingly little scriptural texts explicitly say about their own inspiration (and perhaps more importantly, what they do *not* say about it, i.e., that it is *verbal*);[40] 2) what Scripture appears to inter- and intra-textually evince with respect to its own inspiration *in light of its thoroughgoing cultural embeddedness*;[41] 3) the diachronic development of holy texts into what, over time, came to be accepted as holy *Scripture*;[42] and 4) the historical development of Scripture into what would finally be accepted as a *canon* of Scripture.[43] On the basis of research in patristics, canon forma-

---

of dichotomizing Scripture into teachings and phenomena in Bovell, *Rehabilitating Inerrancy*, chapter six.

38. Ibid., 240.

39. Ibid., 244.

40. Compare John Scullion, *The Theology of Inspiration* (Notre Dame: Fides, 1970), 15: "Neither here [2 Pet 3.14–16] nor anywhere else does the New Testament claim to be itself inspired."

41. For an attempt to illustrate how culturally embedded the Scriptures are along with what implications this may have for evangelical doctrines of Scripture, see Carlos Bovell, "Scriptural Authority and Believing Criticism: The Seriousness of the Evangelical Predicament," *JPS* 3 (2005): 17–27. Online: <http://www.philosophyandscripture.org/Issue3-1/Bovell/Bovell.pdf>.

42. Even inerrantist evangelicals are admitting that autographs for certain portions of the Bible simply never existed. See, for example, Duane L. Christensen, "In Quest of the Autograph of the Book of Jeremiah: A Study of Jeremiah 25 in Relation to Jeremiah 46–51," *JETS* 33 (1990): 145–53.

43. Compare Albert C. Sundberg, Jr., "The Bible Canon and the Christian Doctrine of Inspiration," *Int* 29 (1975): 352: "[O]ur understanding of canonical history entails concomitant and commensurate revision of the doctrine of inspiration."

tion, and NT studies, Craig Allert has almost certainly come to the right conclusion: "Inspiration cannot, therefore, be defined as being located in the individual 'author,' the text, or the 'author' and the text. Inspiration is not seen as something that is inherent in a writing or a writer."[44]

Students, therefore, should not be urged to understand biblical inspiration by taking for its model "prophetic" utterances appearing in the Bible. Unfortunately, this is the most common approach. Morris is typical of evangelical discussions treating the inspiration of Scripture: "the first point to be made is that the OT consistently records words which it claims are God's words."[45] According to Walter Houston, however, in terms of discourse analysis at least, "All that can be said here is that the prophets *claimed* divine authority, and that that claim was contested. Within the terms of the prophetic discourse itself, there is no way of challenging the claim, and we can only continue our analysis, having bypassed the theological question, by pragmatically accepting it."[46] Yet, if evangelical students' acceptance of verbal inspiration of even the prophetic portions of Scripture is for mainly pragmatic reasons, what are they to do with texts in which it *ceases to be pragmatic at all*?[47]

It is only a matter of time before students begin to realize that looking to prophecy for a model for inspiration has some obvious drawbacks: 1) The majority of Scripture does not qualify as "prophecy," making no claim to being God's words. It would be better for students to be told in advance that to claim to be speaking God's words is a well-known genre from antiquity. Prophecy is one of several *literary genres* that appear in the Bible; 2) "Prophecy" is often seen as a special dispensation that God has restricted to an exclusive set of individuals. However, if scriptural inspiration is a special case of the prophetic, why are the Scriptures so thoroughly similar to other writings from antiquity? To take one example, consider

---

44. Craig Allert, "Is a Translation Inspired? The Problems of Verbal Inspiration for Translation and a Proposed Solution," in *Translating the Bible: Problems and Prospects*, ed. S. Porter and R. Hess (London: Sheffield, 1999), 111.

45. Leon Morris, "Biblical Authority and the Concept of Inerrancy," *Chm* 81 (1967): 22. Compare Wayne Grudem, "Scripture's Self-Attestation and the Problem of Formulating a Doctrine of Scripture," in *Scripture and Truth*, ed. D. A. Carson and John Woodbridge (Grand Rapids: Zondervan, 1983), 19–64.

46. Walter Houston, "What Did the Prophets Think They Were Doing? Speech Acts and Prophetic Discourse in the Old Testament," *BibInt* 1 (1993): 179.

47. See Carlos Bovell, *Inerrancy and the Spiritual Formation of Younger Evangelicals* (Eugene, OR: Wipf and Stock, 2007).

Dan McCartney's observation regarding the NT use of the OT: "To appeal to inspiration as somehow 'allowing' the NT writers to do something no one else is allowed to do seems odd in the face of the fact that the apostles were simply interpreting the way their contemporaries did."[48] The "prophecy" model for Scripture tends to keep evangelicals from appreciating how integrally *historical* and *cultural* Scripture turns out to be upon close examination; 3) The diachronic evolution of most Scriptures is so dissimilar from the picture that the prophecy model paints of the composition of Scripture (something as close to dictation as one can reasonably manage in light of biblical "phenomena"[49]) that the prophecy model almost guarantees that students will become disillusioned with their faith once confronted with the Bible's long and complicated documentary history.[50]

6. Illumination or inspiration?

Wyckoff is representative of the evangelical tradition in his conception of illumination as "the idea of the Holy Spirit 'teaching' believers the truths of Scripture."[51] He states that "the 'teacher' model provides the best vehicle of discourse on how the Holy Spirit illuminates Scripture."[52] Despite Wyckoff's disclaimer that no model is comprehensive, evangelicals should have some misgivings about confining such aspects of the Spirit's work to illumination. For my part, I would like to see them re-integrated into the doctrine of inspiration, for as Grenz observed nearly twenty years ago:

---

48. Dan McCartney, "Should We Employ the Hermeneutics of the New Testament Writers," n13. Paper presented at the annual meeting of the Evangelical Theological Society, 2003. Online: <http://www.bible-researcher.com/mccartney1.html>.

49. For Warfield's own grappling with this issue, see A. N. S. Lane, "B.B. Warfield and the Humanity of Scripture," *VE* 16 (1986): 77–94.

50. Michael Grisanti ("Inspiration, Inerrancy, and the OT Canon: The Place of Textual Updating in an Inerrant View of Scripture," *JETS* 44 [2001]: 598) tries to salvage the evangelical prophecy model but unfortunately is left with few historical options: "Finally, I assume that a prophetic figure (having credibility in the Israelite community) introduced these modernizations into a given biblical text." For an introduction to the issues that arise on account of the data, see James A. Sanders, "Understanding the Development of the Biblical Text," in *The Dead Sea Scrolls after Forty Years* (Washington, DC: Biblical Archaeological Society, 1991), 56–74. A more suitable account of prophecy is found in Niels Christian Hvidt, *Christian Prophecy: The Post-Biblical Tradition* (New York: Oxford University Press, 2007).

51. Wyckoff, *Pneuma and Logos*, 129.

52. Ibid., 129.

"The distinction [between inspiration and illumination] can too rigidly separate what is in fact a close relationship between the two dimensions of the Spirit's one activity in Scripture."[53] The Bible's composition, growth and development, transmission and reception are too starkly delineated in evangelical theology. The theological cost of not keeping up with advances in biblical studies is an artificial ramification of the Holy Spirit's involvement surrounding the churches' role in the production, transmission and reception of the holy Scriptures. I am interested in restoring a semblance of unity to the various aspects of the Spirit's work by integrating them into a single theological locus, namely that of in-spiration: the evangelical doctrine of illumination simply does not do justice to how inter-related these various facets ultimately are.

One problem I see with the teacher model of the doctrine of illumination has to do with how common it is for evangelical students to expect the Holy Spirit to teach biblical "truths" from Scripture and that these truths should come in the form of theological propositions. By this model, whenever someone becomes convinced that the Spirit has taught them a given set of propositional truths, all other propositional truths that arise from other disciplines must be forced to conform. They must be made to become compatible with the propositions the believer feels are taught by the Holy Spirit via Scripture.

Another reservation that I have with the teacher model of illumination has to do with how the Holy Spirit has putatively taught different churches throughout history different propositions that cannot all be accepted without contradiction.[54] Some Christians may seek to get around this objection by affirming that he has taught the doctrines found in *their own* church's statement of faith while at the same time denying that the Holy Spirit has taught the doctrines found in *other* churches' statements of faith. Such a position, however, seems a little too convenient to take seriously.[55]

In addition to insulating students from the pluralism that the Holy Spirit authorizes, there is the further concern that the "teacher" model predisposes believers to expect to learn something cognitively every time

---

53. Stanley Grenz, *Theology for the Community of God* (Nashville, TN: Broadman and Holman, 1994), 383.

54. E.g., "Infants receive the Holy Spirit at baptism." "Infants do not receive the Holy Spirit at baptism."

55. Christian Smith has documented how appeals to the Bible do nothing to stem Christian pluralism. See Smith, *The Bible Made Impossible: Why Biblicism Is Not a Truly Evangelical Reading of Scripture* (Grand Rapids: Brazos, 2011).

they read Scripture, supposing that the Bible was given by God mainly to provide believers with either doctrinal information or a propositional description of reality. Certainly there are times when developing cognitive perspectives on faith is appropriate, but *practically speaking* the "teacher" model for biblical illumination reduces Christian faith to cogitating propositions that must be believed in order to receive eternal life (because its adherents presume that the Spirit teaches that such propositions are taught *in Scripture* and must be believed in order to receive eternal life).[56] I have suggested elsewhere that the doctrine of inerrancy has already succumbed to this pitfall, in that evangelical students and scholars are required to affirm that denying inerrancy "set[s] aside the witness of Jesus Christ and of the Holy Spirit and to refuse that submission to the claims of God's own Word which marks true Christian faith."[57]

My concern is that students who live and breathe and have their being in inerrantist communities are being socially conditioned to enjoy and experience only a fraction of what God has made available to them in their exploration of Scripture, for as C. H. Dodd once remarked, "The Bible has suffered from being treated too much as a source of information."[58] Perhaps evangelical students are not achieving as much as they could on behalf of the gospel in terms of making positive contributions to the culture-at-large precisely because of limitations inherent to their understanding of biblical inspiration.[59]

My last reservation has to do with how perspectivally different our "post-Enlightenment" construal of truth is from pre-Enlightenment understandings. For the purposes of this chapter, it must suffice to mention that it was not until developments in seventeenth, eighteenth, and nineteenth-century philosophy and biblical criticism that post-Reformation

---

56. Compare A. T. B. McGowan's concerns in McGowan, *The Divine Spiration of Scripture: Challenging Evangelical Perspectives* (Nottingham: Apollos, 2007).

57. "Preface to the Chicago Statement on Biblical Inerrancy." Many parts of conservative Evangelicalism incorporate this understanding of Scripture into its broader culture, negatively affecting students. See Bovell, *Rehabilitating Inerrancy*.

58. C. H. Dodd, *The Authority of the Bible* (rev. ed.; New York: Harper and Row, 1960), 270.

59. Consider a post on the blog, *Church and Culture*, run by James Emery White, a theology faculty member of Gordon-Conwell Seminary, for example. In an entry entitled, "The Stupidity of Inerrancy and a Long Winter," White laments a "longing for absolutes" and "a desire for certainty" among teens and twenty-somethings and recommends inerrancy as a way to fill the void! Online: <http://www.churchandculture.org/Blog.asp?ID=396>.

thinking within conservative Protestantism developed lines of thought that have culminated in present-day fixations on whether believers are upholding Scripture as being historically or scientifically "true."[60] As Wolterstorff has pointed out, the word "true" has enjoyed a wide range of uses throughout history. Evangelical theologians, describing how the Bible as God's word has to be "true,"[61] have shown a disproportionate amount of interest in defining truth as "what is the case." In the meantime, truth as "rectitude," truth as "proper functioning," truth as "having to be the case," and truth as "measuring up" have not received the consideration they merit for conceiving how Scripture is true. When contemporary thinking in the Anglo-American tradition restricted its discussion to the truth/falsity of assertions, evangelical theologians and philosophers were only too eager to follow suit when they talked about scriptural truth.[62]

Another important point to consider is that it was not until 1710, in Giambattista Vico's work, *On the Ancient Wisdom of the Italians Taken from the Origins of the Latin Language*, that the dictum, "the criterion and rule of the true is to have made it," was first proposed. Richard Campbell explains

> we must interpret [Vico's] maker's knowledge principle as insisting that in order to understand an artifact, one needs to know *what* the thing is, i.e. its form. But to know that requires that one know *how* the form (genus, mode) organizes all the "elements" from which the thing has been synthesized, i.e. arranged and put together.[63]

---

60. John Frame illustrates the evangelical ethos. Not until someone convincingly shows that "God *cannot* guarantee the continuing truthfulness of written sentences" will he seriously entertain a non-inerrantist proposal (such as the one put forth by Karl Barth). See Frame, "The Spirit and the Scriptures," in *Hermeneutics, Authority, and Canon*, ed. D. A. Carson and John D. Woodbridge (Grand Rapids: Zondervan, 1986), 225.

61. Norman Geisler ("An Evaluation of McGowen's [sic!] View on the Inspiration of Scripture," *BibSac* 167 [2010]: 21, 22) continues to insist, for example, that "the Bible claims for itself . . . that truth must be judged by its correspondence to the facts" and that "[t]he correspondence view of truth is the one the Bible embraces."

62. See Nicholas Wolterstorff, "True Words," in *But Is It All True? The Bible and the Question of Truth*, ed. A. G. Padgett and P. R. Keifert (Grand Rapids: Eerdmans, 2006), 41–42. Wolterstorff appropriates speech act theory in an attempt to move emphasis away from assertions and toward what he calls the "illocutionary stance" of the Bible. See Wolterstorff, *Divine Discourse: Philosophical Reflections on the Claim that God Speaks* (New York: Cambridge University Press, 1995).

63. Richard Campbell, *Truth and Historicity* (New York: Oxford University Press, 1992), 259.

The *verum/factum* principle, as Campbell calls it, developed out of Vico's reading of Hobbes. The original context for Vico's understanding that humans "make" truth was informed by Christian, theological speculation.[64] In fact, among the earliest applications of the *verum/factum* principle were to the interpretation of the Bible and the formulation of a doctrine of Scripture. When critics of inerrancy claim that inerrancy is a modern construct, they are complaining about how uncritically evangelicals have accepted and applied this definition of "truth" to their doctrine of Scripture. All this to say that for twenty-first-century believers there is a fundamental tension between "truth" and "making" that past luminaries would not have thought to reckon with, and evangelical doctrines of inerrancy, like the Chicago Statement, fail to acknowledge this. Hermeneutical conclusions drawn at Vatican II help illustrate the point:

> From all this it follows that the exegete must engage in the art of form criticism as a method of reaching some understanding of *how* the Holy Spirit was at work among the people of God, guiding its life and enlightening the minds of prophet, apostle and evangelist for the work of creating the sacred text as the authoritative witness to God's saving activity.[65]

In order to understand what Scripture is and how it can be *true*, it is imperative we learn whatever we can about how the Scriptures were *made*. Evangelical inerrantism has been very reluctant to accept this, insisting that an account for how Scriptures were made be presented that validates their understanding of how Scripture is true.

In short, these four considerations 1) overemphasizing theological propositions, 2) overlooking diversity, 3) overestimating the cognitive aspects of faith, and 4) underappreciating the semantic range of "true," cumulatively suggest that evangelical doctrines of illumination effectively tear asunder what God has joined together. As an alternate, I propose constructing a doctrine of inspiration that covers all phases of the formation and reception of Scripture throughout the church's history.

---

64. Ibid., 259. Interestingly, Campbell considers Vico's "deep connection between truth and making" to be a modern variation of Anselm's truth as doing. Miner is another scholar who insists that "*Verum-factum*, as Vico understands it, is inscribed within a theological metaphysics." See Robert Miner, *Truth in the Making: Creative Knowledge in Theology and Philosophy* (New York: Routledge, 2004), 100.

65. Martin H. Scharlemann, "Roman Catholic Biblical Interpretation," in *Festschrift to Honor F. Wilbur Gingrich, Lexicographer, Scholar, Teacher, and Committed Christian Layman*, ed. E. H. Barth and R. E. Cocroft (Leiden: E. J. Brill, 1972), 218, emphasis added.

7. Conclusion

In John 7:39, the evangelist explains how the disciples finally came to understand what Jesus was talking about when he referred to "rivers of living waters flowing from within him." The evangelist's candid retrospection reads as follows: "He said this in reference to the Spirit that those who came to believe in him were to receive. There was, of course, no Spirit yet, because Jesus had not yet been glorified." What I am recommending is the incorporation of the Johannine hermeneutical premise—"Of course we didn't understand! We didn't have the Spirit yet and we *couldn't* have had it since he hadn't yet been glorified!"—into a truly historical account of biblical inspiration. The fourth Gospel is insistent that only *after* Jesus was glorified were the disciples infused with the Spirit, only *after* Jesus was glorified were the disciples spiritually equipped to breathe life into Scripture. The disciples were viscerally in-spired with the Spirit, directly from the mouth of Jesus.

As we construct a doctrine of biblical inspiration, I urge that more attention be given to how the disciples' spiritual in-fusion, according to John's Gospel, enabled them to breathe life into Scripture, i.e., to receive Jesus' own words in ways that gave them life, in ways that made the Scriptures as a whole—via Jesus' own understanding of them[66]—come alive. Jesus' words could really be "words of eternal life," since they have as their source the fountain of living water, *a source they now shared with Jesus himself*. Once the disciples had this living water flowing out of them, the words Jesus spoke, particularly his hermeneutical outlook, came alive to the disciples. Their ability to bring the Scriptures to life was made possible by the coordination of the Spirit in Scripture with the Spirit now alive in the "spirits" of the disciples, a process I am inclined to call "hermeneutics."[67] The picture is one in which the Spirit in believers meets the Spirit in Scripture, *enlivening both*: both are divinely in-spired.

To some evangelical readers, my proposal may seem inherently unevangelical, but they should keep in mind that I am deliberately seeking

---

66. Jean-Luc Marion ("They Recognized Him; And He Became Invisible to Them," *ModT* 18 [2002]: 149) describes Jesus as the "sole 'exegete of God (*ekeinos exêgêsato*)' (John 1:18) to interpret the Scripture that God inspired in order to announce Him to humans as the fulfillment of all his promises."

67. Marion goes on to observe: "The text will tell us nothing more of this exegesis, other than that it made the disciples understand that 'it was fitting that the Christ should suffer in order to enter into his glory' (v. 26)." Marion is reflecting on Luke 24:13–25. See ibid., 149.

*an evangelical corrective.*⁶⁸ When I turned to compare my ideas regarding inspiration with those appearing in non-evangelical traditions, it became clear to me just how badly evangelicals are in need of correction on this matter. I have already made reference to changes brought about in Roman Catholic thought in the wake of Vatican II.⁶⁹ In addition, Orthodox theologians have traditionally been open to the idea that hermeneutics is, in large measure, what makes the Bible come alive:⁷⁰

> "Tradition is the permanent vitality of Holy Scripture, *its living meaning* . . ."⁷¹
>
> "Tradition is the life of the Holy Spirit in the Church."⁷²
>
> "For inspiration is a *global* phenomenon that encompasses not only the author, but also the *interpreter* of Scripture. . . . St. Paul's affirmation to Timothy, 'all Scripture is inspired' (II Tim 3:16), should be understood as referring to this global inspirational activity of the Holy Spirit."⁷³

A. T. Hanson once pointed out that "we are in a different position for ever to [the earliest Christians]" since we also count *their* writings as

---

68. If Geisler's ("Evaluation," 37–38) intransigence is representative, it will take time for evangelicals to accept, much less come to terms with, the thought that God never provided an "original Bible": "With Scripture it was essential to have an original that was perfect since a perfect God cannot make an imperfect original. . . . God produced a perfect original Bible . . . Two premises are clearly taught in Scripture: God cannot make errors, and the original Bible is the Word of God."

69. Also relevant are Scharlemann's ("Roman Catholic," 213) parenthetical remarks: "Roman Catholic Biblical scholars are learning well the lessons of *Formgeschichte* and of *Redaktionsgeschichte*. These exegetical pursuits have tended to reinforce the concept of tradition with which that Church has lived for centuries."

70. Catholic theologian Anthony Meredith (*The Theology of Tradition* [Notre Dame, IL: Fides, 1970], 58–61) also commends the Orthodox Church for having "a very deep conviction of the all-pervasive action of the Holy Spirit." Everett Kalin ("The Inspired Community: A Glance at Canon History," *CTM* 42 [1971]: 542) reports that indeed this was the basic outlook of the early church: "In fact, the inspiration that the fathers ascribed to the Scriptures is only one facet of what they regarded as a much wider inspiration, for the fathers saw the inspiring activity of the Holy Spirit at work in many aspects of the church's life."

71. Kallistos Ware, "Tradition, the Bible and the Holy Spirit," *Epiph* 11 (1991): 14, emphasis added.

72. Ware, "Tradition," 9. Ware is citing Vladimir Lossky in this quote.

73. John Breck, *The Power of the Word in the Worshipping Church* (Crestwood, NY: St. Vladimir's, 1986), 43–44.

part of our Scriptures (i.e., the NT).[74] But let this not obscure a more basic similarity: Our location in redemptive history is such that the Holy Spirit intercedes for our spirits in our efforts to read words we cannot (spiritually) comprehend.[75] This, I suggest, is part of the one divine action that I want to call "inspiration." To paraphrase Paul, he who searches our hearts and minds understands the mind of the Spirit of Scripture (i.e., its christological significance) and mediates to us divinely intended meanings as Spirit-filled, post-resurrection believers. *This is all the work of the same Spirit.* When it comes to inspiration, both the Scriptures and believers are divinely inspired. With both "Spirits" coordinately operative throughout the organic, inspirational process—which includes both the formation and reception of the Christian Bible—all Scripture can properly be conceived as hermeneutically God-breathed.

---

74. Hanson, *New Testament Interpretation*, 18. Interestingly enough, according to Kalin, although the early church believed that all Scripture is inspired, they would not have agreed that that all non-Scripture is un-inspired. See Kalin, "Inspired Community," 542.

75. Compare Origen, *Princ.* 2.7.2.

Biblical Inspiration

Responses

The Doctrine of Inspiration and the Dead Sea Scrolls

George J. Brooke

CARLOS R. BOVELL HAS written an intriguing study in which he uses his particular reading of the Fourth Gospel as the basis for an argument that strongly encourages modern Christian believers to take seriously their own participation in the construction of the inspiration of Scripture. We should be aware that there might be something of the chicken and the egg in the circularity of his argument, using Scripture to interpret how Scripture should be interpreted. Nevertheless, the aim of his study, he says, is to account for "the role the Holy Spirit plays in composition, transmission, and reception of Scripture by expanding the evangelical notion of biblical inspiration to encompass more than just the authors and the texts. I am seeking to integrate the formative and communicative aspects of Scripture into a more comprehensive doctrine of inspiration." Or again: "The picture that I have in mind is one where the Spirit in each of us 'reaches out' to the Spirit in Scripture, making it come alive."

With suitable caveats, I would like to buy into his approach in a qualified way and particularly to say something about the transmission and reception of Scripture in the pre-canonical period that might throw some light on any modern construction of the doctrine of inspiration. To my knowledge, the scrolls that come from the Dead Sea region have yet to be factored systematically into any kind of formulation of a Christian doctrine of inspiration. This short note is written as encouragement to Bovell's approach to the text of Scripture and, as someone who has worked with the Dead Sea Scrolls for forty years, to push things a little further still. I have five brief points to throw into the discussion that arise from research into the Dead Sea Scrolls, especially those found in the eleven caves at and near Qumran.

First, it is clear that at the time of Jesus and the authors of the New Testament books, and certainly in the few generations before them, the text of Scripture, that is, both the content and the form of the text of the Old Testament was not entirely stable. In fact, it can of course be shown that the text of the Bible has never been entirely stable; that fact is what reveals approaches like that of *The Bible Code* to be entirely arbitrary, to the point of being nonsense. More seriously, some dismiss the variants amongst Hebrew manuscripts of the Hebrew Bible (and also amongst the New Testament manuscripts) as of little significance, but to my mind, they need to be given some room in the discussion. On the one hand, it is true that the manuscripts from the Qumran caves that contain copies of those works that were to find their way into Jewish and Christian canons indicate strongly the continuity between the complete medieval manuscripts of the books of the Hebrew Bible and the time of Hillel and Jesus. Nevertheless, it also has to be acknowledged that no single manuscript copy of a scriptural work from the Qumran caves agrees letter for letter with the later rabbinic forms of the text; some are indeed very close, but others represent different editions of the books concerned.

What is to be made of the textual variety that is apparent in the scriptural manuscripts found in the Qumran caves? To my mind, any kind of initially defensive reaction that wants to identify the variations as errors is certainly inappropriate. Some few variations might indeed be errors, as is also acknowledged for a few items in the rabbinic bibles too, but the vast amount of variation is much more positive evidence for how authoritative texts were viewed before they were supposedly fixed in some canonical form. In the pre-canonical period, to which I consider Jesus also belongs, we now know that scribes actively participated in the transmission process of the authoritative texts for which they found themselves responsible. I consider that many modern translators have found themselves with a similar sense of participatory responsibility. Scribal transmitters of texts, even modern translators, are very much part of what Bovell has identified as attesting the place of the Spirit in communities of faith.

Second, there is an instant corollary to the first point. Let us draw out the significance of the fact that, at the time of Jesus and today, there is more than one edition of several books of the Hebrew Bible. For example, it is now clear to most interpreters of the evidence that the form of Jeremiah in the Greek translation used by the orthodox churches is both shorter and also in several places arranged in a different order from that found in the

The Doctrine of Inspiration and the Dead Sea Scrolls

rabbinic bibles which, since the sixteenth century, have generally formed the basis of Protestant translations of the text. Amongst the Qumran caves there are Hebrew manuscripts that agree with both forms of Jeremiah; in the first century BCE there were two forms of the work in circulation in Palestine. Which one is to be taken as *inspired*? Or, put more frankly, do Eastern or Western Christians use the *inspired* version? Here is where Carlos Bovell's approach is surely required. It is not just a faithful community, but various faithful communities that bring the text alive. I am convinced that there is no reason to doubt that both forms of Jeremiah are *inspired*. No one church can claim an exclusive privilege of inspiration, as Bovell points out lucidly and convincingly. The evidence does not allow it.

Third, there is the matter of the link between prophecy and inspiration. Much ink has been used in Christian writings on this matter. It is probably inappropriate to think that there is much new to be said, but one matter comes strikingly to mind. In the Jewish sect, part of which resided at Qumran in the first centuries BCE and CE, a group of learned scribes produced a set of running commentaries on various scriptural books that they considered prophetically significant, including Isaiah, some of the Twelve, and the Psalms. Those compositions have become known as the continuous pesharim, because the Hebrew term *pesher*, commonly rendered as "interpretation," is used as part of a technical formula that connects the scriptural lemma with the comments that follow: "its interpretation concerns" or "the interpretation of the matter is." None of this might seem particularly remarkable, except that one of these commentaries states explicitly that the prophet who originally was supposed to have received the oracle did not know all the meaning of what God had given to him; rather, God had now made known to the community's inspired Teacher "all the mysteries of the words of his servants the prophets" (1QpesherHabakkuk VII, 4–5). God-given insight, so these ancient writers claim, rests neither with the prophetic author nor in the text, but with the one to whom God has made things known. If the whole community sets about studying the texts and their interpretations, as the sectarian compositions recommend for at least a third of every night (1QRule of the Community VI, 7–8), then such God-given insight can also reside with them.

Fourth, if there is indeed such a thing as divinely inspired interpretation of authoritative Scriptures, then how is the community of faith able to recognize such interpretation for what it claims to be? The continuous pesharim, these running commentaries, disclose to their audiences that the interpretations that they offer are not arbitrary or random, not produced solely for the moment. Rather only the most highly trained scriptural experts can loose the Scripture to disclose its meaning. The astute reader or hearer of the interpretation can readily recognize its veracity, because the interpreter and audience share a set of interpretative tools that have been honed over many generations. The suitable application of these tools permits for appropriate interpretations to be offered. And a couple of features of the interpretation are worth noting: first, there is the fact that any one scriptural passage can have multiple meanings, and second, amongst those multiple meanings no special priority is assigned to a literalist approach to the text, even though the plain meaning of the text has to be taken seriously.

Fifth, I am constantly struck by the role of providence in all this. The riches of the Dead Sea Scrolls are quite remarkable, as is readily recognized by the thousands who turn out to see them when a few are exhibited from time to time. Their scriptural manuscripts provide us with information about the state of the Hebrew texts of the books of the Old Testament that is a thousand years older than what was hitherto available; likewise, there is much that has been gleaned from the wealth of other compositions in Hebrew and Aramaic. All that has come to light since 1947, since the Second World War. With something of a long perspective, I consider that the same period of sixty years or so has also produced some of the most vocal, doctrinaire, and hardened views of Scripture in some Christian circles. All the new evidence, it seems to me, puts narrow doctrines of scriptural inspiration in a new light; there is a kind of divine sense of humour in all this. Not least, the new evidence of scriptural variety and vivacity in Judaism at the time of Jesus shows how it is so very important for the faith communities, both Jewish and Christian, variously to take responsibility for their handling of Scripture. Scripture should not be understood as a fixed and finalized matter, done and dusted, at risk of being idolized, especially at risk of being quoted out of context. It is a lively affair and those who handle the texts of Scripture are handling things that can indeed be understood as matters of life and death. This sense of multiple community responsibility for the tradition means that there has never been a greater need for the skilled interpreter who might both seek to "understand" Scripture, but also be willing to "stand under" its variegated authority with humility, and who will also be willing to take into account the views of others from other communities, even other communities of faith. Those who think that they have all the answers about the text of Scripture and how it should be viewed have probably got the question wrong, or at least have not appreciated the character of the data about Scripture and its interpretation that the Dead Sea Scrolls have allowed us to see afresh.

What is a Doctrine of Scriptural Inspiration *For*?
A Dialogue with Carlos Bovell

Richard S. Briggs

CARLOS BOVELL ARGUES THAT "Scripture is hermeneutically God-breathed."[1] I take it that his thesis has a positive and a negative element. The former is that all Scripture is useful: the Scriptures are "ready *to be made alive*" (3), and to yield to newly Spirit-inspired readers in the manner of those interlocutors of John's gospel who acquire "a new hermeneutical capacity" in the post-resurrection world (12). The latter, the negative part, is that evangelical doctrines of inspiration typically limit inspiration to some inherent property of the text, and separate off the Spirit's work of "illumination" to some separate stage. Bovell instead seeks a "unity" in our understanding of the Spirit's work in and through Scripture: a doctrine of Scripture which covers "all phases of the formation and reception of Scripture" (21).

I am not sure that his overall title captures what is at stake here: "hermeneutically God-breathed" turns out not to mean that the God-breathing was effected in some hermeneutical manner, so much as that, in matters of hermeneutics, the breath of God need never be far away. I wonder if the phrase that would capture this point is "all Scripture is God-breathed such that it is ready for (God-breathed) hermeneutical endeavor," (though I grant that this is a less elegant phrase for a title). The point is that the hermeneutics, as much as the production of the text in the first place, takes place in God's economy, under the rubric of God's inspiring work.

There is much to applaud in this proposal, which offers evident benefits over some other formulations. In particular, it is evident that Bovell

1. I am grateful to Carlos R. Bovell for the invitation to respond to his chapter.

is self-consciously seeking to provide an alternative to what he describes as, without qualification, "The Evangelical Doctrine of Inspiration." It is debatable as to whether there is only one such evangelical doctrine (singular), or whether there might not be a range of evangelical articulations of a doctrine of inspiration. It is at least plausible to suggest that what Bovell means by this phrase is something like a traditionally quite conservative evangelical view of inspiration. But in any case, he sets out to provide an "alternate picture" and "an evangelical corrective."

One may grant that his own view is a considerable improvement on what he takes as the standard evangelical picture, largely for the very reasons he offers along the way. What I would like to do here, however, is to suggest that for all its merits, Bovell's approach to the inspiration of Scripture ends up being an account which is still largely shaped and in some ways constrained by the very categories against which it is reacting. Bovell has taken as read the starting point of a typical evangelical account of inspiration, and has asked how it might be supplemented to do better justice to Scripture's own witness of the continuing work of the Spirit in interpretation. By way of friendly dialogue with where he ends up, I wonder if I might suggest that one could do even better justice to a doctrine of inspiration by starting somewhere else in the first place. In other words, what Bovell sees as a "corrective" is, in the end, constrained in some ways by not digging down deep enough to root out the problems associated with thinking of inspiration as a property of the so-called "original text."

I will try to elucidate what I have in mind by briefly considering inspiration in dialogue with a range of other theological concerns, which do not take their initial orientation from this desire to "correct" an already articulated version of the doctrine.

Inspiration in Dialogue with Exegesis

I have elsewhere attempted a low-key discussion of just what a doctrine of inspiration suitably shaped by Scripture itself might look like.[2] There, I started not with any traditional doctrine of inspiration, evangelical or otherwise, but with attention to those texts which might be thought to bear upon the question of how God is at work in the "breathing out" of scriptural

---

2. See Richard S. Briggs, *Reading the Bible Wisely. An Introduction to Taking Scripture Seriously*, rev. ed. (Eugene, OR: Cascade, 2011), 67–77, on "The Inspiration of Scripture and the Breath of God."

texts—not as some kind of putative "scriptural proof" that this is how it must be, obviously, but more out of a conviction that our own reasoning on this topic will be wiser if we allow it to be shaped by comparable scriptural reflections themselves. I ended up suggesting that there is not a lot one needs to say about inspiration if one starts from a passage like 2 Timothy 3—the reference to inspiration here really is a passing reference. What it secures is that "all Scripture is useful" (for a range of activities such as teaching, rebuking, and so forth). It seems clear that hardly anything in 2 Timothy 3 offers any cashing-out of "God-breathed" in terms of any properties of the text—possibly "holy" (3:15) is one such property, and indeed has traditionally been seen as one by those who publish, buy, and read a "Holy Bible." "Useful" is of course the other, but neither of these labels nor properties packages up with them a set of claims about the content of Scripture.

Clearly, one cannot settle the nuances of a doctrine of inspiration by attending to 2 Timothy 3, but I do argue in my own discussion of the matter that these kinds of observation can be extended to a fuller account than one driven just by this passage.[3] In other words, there are various scriptural pointers to how we might best think of the inspiring work of God in and through scriptural texts—a claim with which I think Bovell would basically agree.

But, as one might put it, the doctrine is in the details. So I must register some slight concern that the particular hermeneutical moves which Bovell makes with biblical texts may be driven more by a desire to get from his starting point to his conclusions rather than by exegesis as such. One particular claim of his essay is that—under the model afforded by John's gospel—it is readers possessed by the Spirit who are able to discern Christ in the Scriptures, which Scriptures were presumably opaque beforehand in this respect. There is surely something important in such a claim: as he says, "the Spirit in each of us 'reaches out' to the Spirit in Scripture, making it come alive" (12). Something like this may well be said about the famous passage of the disciples on the road to Emmaus in Luke 24, meeting Jesus and being driven to reconsider Scripture, while yet of course, one of the things which Jesus is doing along that walk is showing them that it is Scripture which points to him.[4]

---

3. Briggs, *Reading the Bible Wisely*, 73–77.

4. My own discussion of this dynamic is in *Reading the Bible Wisely*, 9–19, but it is a common point to make with regard to the relevance of Luke 24 to Christian hermeneutics.

What is a Doctrine of Scriptural Inspiration For?

What I find less helpful in the model he draws out of John's gospel is the, apparently, rather unconstrained emphasis on the Spirit-endowed hermeneutical capacity in the reader. It may well be that I have not fully grasped what John himself is trying to do, but I wonder whether one of the reasons why Bovell is able to discern this model here is in turn related to John's own pressing concerns with contrasting the life of the Spirit with that of "the Jews" (*hoi Judaioi*). There were doubtless reasons for John's emphasis, although the price of this casual identification has been high in the history of Christian-Jewish relationships,[5] such that one might today try to point in a helpful direction by rendering the term "Jewish leaders" (or perhaps "Judaeans") to indicate that it was a specific set of people in a specific situation who were the problem, rather than "the Jews" *per se*. Does Bovell's attempt to draw lessons about a generic doctrine of inspiration unhelpfully broaden this emphasis out again to a flat contrast between either having the Spirit or finding Scripture opaque? Is it more helpful to suggest that (a) this may occasionally be exactly the pair of contrasting options available, but (b) more generally, there is an interplay between the work of the Spirit and the pressure of the text, such that (c) it might be more normal to suggest that what one has is a hermeneutical spiral between the Spirit-inspired reader and the Spirit-inspired text? And further, a doctrine of the Spirit's work would, presumably at some point, want to suggest that even readings offered by those not thinking themselves indebted to the Spirit might still be materially achieved by the work of the (unacknowledged) Spirit.

It may well be that Bovell would grant all this. Perhaps my question is only whether his reading of John has been overly shaped by trying to react against a notion of inspiration being in the text, rather than asking more broadly how the Spirit and Scripture are shown in inter-play in the fourth gospel. And it is interesting to ask what the implications might be of observing that in the very act of writing down this account of the matter, John is surely intending to clarify that there are good reasons why one *should* allow the scriptural text to have its way after all, including (henceforth) his own account.

---

5. For one helpful account among many of what is at stake see Stephen Motyer, *Your Father the Devil? A New Approach to John and "the Jews"* (Carlisle: Paternoster, 1997).

BIBLICAL INSPIRATION—RESPONSES

Inspiration in Dialogue with Canon

A second dialogue which I think might be overly shaped by the assumptions of the piece relates to the nature of the text which is being discussed: the canonical text of Scripture. I shall come at this point by way of an observation about the framework of Bovell's argument.

To this particular British reader, there is a striking oddity about Bovell's paper. His discussion of "inspiration"—of the "God-breathed" dimension of Scripture—is clearly intended to address evangelical concerns. But as it proceeds, it appears that the focus of such concerns is largely some sort of doctrine of "inerrancy," with a concern about propositions. Now on the one hand, it is fine if Bovell wants to discuss inerrancy, but it is not clear to me why a discussion of inspiration needs to take this path. Bovell has some form in this area. Just before accepting the invitation to write this response, I had been invited to review a book he edited which was advertised as being about the *authority* of Scripture.[6] The advertised concerns struck me as productive and worthy of exploration. But on attending to the book, I discovered that it was, in fact, a collection of discussions about inerrancy. Again, in and of itself, that need not have been a problem, but what has a doctrine of inerrancy to do with the question of authority? All manner of people, texts, and rulings are authoritative in life (even church life) without being inerrant. Why the gravitational pull of this discussion—apparently sucking in consideration of inspiration and authority across the board?

What might one say about inerrancy if asked to address it directly?[7] Perhaps very little, and this is because the doctrine of inerrancy is a response, at least in most articulations I have encountered, to an ill-formed question about what Scripture is for. It reminds me of having to write un-

---

6. Carlos R. Bovell (ed.), *Interdisciplinary Perspectives on the Authority of Scripture. Historical, Biblical, and Theoretical Perspectives* (Eugene, OR: Pickwick Publications, 2011).

7. There may, perhaps, be a need for a thoughtful theological account of inerrancy which is written neither particularly to defend or critique it. Most of what I say here relates to my experience of encountering it as a doctrine held by self-defined evangelical Christians, but I note, too, the interesting collection of essays from a (conservative) Roman Catholic perspective in *Letter and Spirit* 6 (2010), under the heading "For the Sake of Our Salvation: The Truth and Humility of God's Word." This is a lengthy issue (432 pages) containing almost 20 essays on the inspiration of Scripture, many of which defend inerrancy as the doctrine of Scripture appropriate to Roman Catholicism. It would be interesting to see how (Protestant) evangelical defenders of inerrancy might receive such a defense.

dergraduate philosophy essays about whether or not I had stopped beating my wife. The problem is that the framework is skewed. *If* one grants that making statements about what is or is not (or was or was not) the case is the purpose of (some? all?) scriptural statements, and perhaps that all scriptural sentences incorporate some kind of proposition capable of being true or false, well then one could, in theory, have a meaningful discussion about whether all the resultant claims are without "error." In practice, such a discussion might not get past the problem of what counts as error, and (equally) who gets to define what it is: Is it Ezekiel? Theophilus? Or Calvin? Or Rob Bell? Or again, is it the philosophers, even those who disavow belief in God—although it is hard to imagine how that might qualify them to be *more* of an authority on the right categories for reading Christian Scripture? Even on such assumptions, it seems to me that inerrancy is problematic, and not just because of the various notorious "problem passages" for it, regarding chronology, geography, and so forth. Rather, it is problematic because in many and various places (and most strikingly in its accounts of the crucifixion and resurrection), Scripture turns out to be remarkably focused on giving multiple and different accounts with little concern as to whether or not they are capable of being understood as affirming the same things about what was the case.

But since almost none of the conditions for this discussion may in fact be granted, it ends up being one that we cannot meaningfully pursue. I thus find myself unimpressed by defenses of inerrancy, but also, in this particular sense, unimpressed by flat assertions that Scripture is errant either. Faced with a Joshua-like interrogation to answer the question: "Are you for or against inerrancy?," I want to respond "Neither, but I *am* here to trust Scripture, and to read it as appropriately authoritative." Those for and against it are, I think, both equally in thrall to the facilitating set of assumptions which are required to render the discussion meaningful, and this set of assumptions is theologically problematic.[8]

I wonder, then, if Bovell rather conflates two different aspects of an argument against a particular ("evangelical") view of inspiration. One concerns its limitations within the framework in which it makes sense—such matters as whether 2 Timothy 3 supports it, or whether it delivers the appropriate results with regard to the longed-for matters concerning

---

8. A most helpful mapping of frameworks within which different positions are taken about assertions, facts, and so forth, remains Nancey Murphy and James Wm. McClendon, Jr, "'Distinguishing Modern and Postmodern Theologies," *Modern Theology* 5 (1989): 191–214.

"salvation."⁹ The other concerns whether the framework within which it is posited is the best, or most constructive, or most theologically appropriate one. And here I want to locate the key issue in whether, or how, the biblical text is treated as canon.

Let us consider a rather significant sentence early in Bovell's piece: "If these historical-critical findings are correct, the evangelical position of restricting inspiration to the texts and their authors may need to be rethought" (4). This seems to be the claim that there are ways in which the proper evangelical doctrine of Scripture is beholden to historical-critical findings about the biblical text. This is a clear example of an argument which presumes that the appropriate framework for the discussion is in place, and if only we get the details right, the doctrine will fall in line. I think what has happened here is that Bovell can see, rightly, that it will not do to restrict inspiration to the text alone, and thus—as we saw—he goes on to appeal to scriptural examples where the Spirit is at work in readers/believers. But of course, Scripture was not in the business of opposing modern evangelical (or other) doctrines of inspiration, and there is little evidence that anyone in the ancient world thought in terms of the inspiring work of the Spirit being an inherent property of texts (as Bovell would doubtless agree).

As a result, Bovell's broadly helpful intuitions about what one can profitably say about the inspiring work of the Spirit are allied to a polemical agenda about what one should avoid saying (i.e. that the text itself is inspired), such that some traditional affirmations about the importance of what the text says are unhelpfully swept away. More precisely, it is not that the mistake of traditional evangelical doctrines of inspiration was to focus on the text at the expense of the Spirit-filled reader; but rather, that it actually focused on the originating context of the text, as is clear from the widespread focus given to such matters as identifying the author, or the point of composition, its date and location, and so forth. Such evangelical approaches, in this regard, share something significant in common with many kinds of historically and critically focused enquiry: they collapse "what the text says" into an account of the text's background assumptions and concerns, which is not irrelevant, but is, at best, only partially adequate. Now, since it is true that what the text says (and indeed what God says through the text) continues to grow and develop all through the development of the

---

9. According to Bovell, "much rides on a correct view of the inspiration and authority of the Bible, and for some believers, this includes their salvation" (6), which, if true, would surely indicate that something has gone very wrong indeed.

canon and on into church history, this point looks a lot like a claim that the Spirit's work needs to be relocated to the reader from the text, *but only if the presenting framework is such that one thinks "text" as focus requires us to talk about the originating context only*. To speak of the text as inspired, in the full richness of what it means to speak of the text saying anything at all, is the purpose of a properly canonical approach, in which the "reality" of which the text speaks may or may not be "what happened" (or "what was the case"), but is, in any event, the very reality which the text raises for consideration by an attentive reader.[10] This is not the place to attempt a full account of what a doctrine of inspiration looks like on these working assumptions, but conveniently for our purposes such an account already exists: it is provided by Stephen Chapman as part of the work of the *Scripture and Hermeneutics* project which has sought in recent years to rethink some of the frameworks and assumptions behind a properly *faithful* and suitably theological approach to Scripture. At the climax of his argument about inspiration, Chapman writes this:

> ... the claim of inspiration is a public confession by members of the Christian community that they are committed to reading and interpreting Scripture as being entirely meaningful; i.e. that *every part* of the canon, under the right conditions (e.g. careful scrutiny, spiritual discernment, faithful proclamation, communal testing), has the ability to express the will of God.[11]

If one were to take the conversation on from there, one would end up discussing what count as the right conditions, and that—I wager—would be a more useful set of discussions to be having than those which typically relate to the originating contexts of the texts, let alone comparisons of chronological or geographical markers.

One way to summarize what Chapman is getting at here is that inspiration is indeed a work of God in the production and preservation of

---

10. Biblical narrative is thus "realistic" in this sense, as observed by Hans Frei in his seminal argument about *The Eclipse of Biblical Narrative: A Study in Eighteenth and Nineteenth Century Hermeneutics* (New Haven: Yale University Press, 1974), 1–16 and throughout.

11. Stephen B. Chapman, "Reclaiming Inspiration for the Bible," in *Canon and Biblical Interpretation*, ed. C. Bartholomew, S. Hahn, R. Parry, et al. (Carlisle: Paternoster, 2006), 167–206, here 188. At one point, Chapman cuts through a lengthy debate about "original meaning" with this well-judged observation: "The problem, of course, is that texts *always* mean something they never could have meant to their authors and (first) readers!" (183).

Scripture, and as such, it will indeed include ways in which the text is itself inspired as readers read it, but overall, there is no need to limit inspiration to any one stage of God's superintendence of Scripture (in this case: the originating moment of the text). This happens to deal rather nicely with the recognition that many texts have no singular originating moment, and some indeed have no original "autograph," a point to which Bovell rightly alludes.[12] Since the inspiring work of the Spirit extends back beyond such moments, and onwards into the reading and reception of the texts too, one might expect that it matters little whether there was such an originating moment. While for some kinds of text (such as an epistle occasioned by a particular crisis) it will be of immense hermeneutical help to grasp the nature of the originating context (the crisis itself, say), this must not be confused with the notion that the inspired text must have been the work of a particular moment. All of this, I think, fits with what Bovell wants to affirm, but the kind of rethinking which is needed to get to this understanding of Scripture goes deeper than supplementing traditional evangelical concerns with sharper historical-critical findings, and moves on to a more theologically attuned reading of the canon as the context in which Scripture says what it says, not what we would interpret it as saying in order to illuminate our own contexts.

Inspiration in Dialogue with Doctrine

I come finally to the most doctrinal of these reflections: what is a doctrine of inspiration for? I am mindful of a striking, recent engagement between a biblical scholar and a systematician regarding the project of moving "beyond the Bible" towards doctrine.[13] Thus, on the one hand, Howard Marshall urged biblical scholars out beyond the limits of attention to the Bible so that doctrine could be brought into the picture. And in response, Kevin Vanhoozer suggested, among other things, that this was all well and good, but what does one mean by "doctrine"?[14] Bovell, on a somewhat related

---

12. See several of the helpful essays gathered in Vincent Bacote, Laura C. Miguélez and Dennis L. Okholm (eds.), *Evangelicals & Scripture. Tradition, Authority and Hermeneutics* (Downers Grove, IL: IVP, 2004).

13. I. Howard Marshall, *Beyond the Bible. Moving from Scripture to Theology* (Grand Rapids: Baker Academic, 2004), a book which contains "responses" from Kevin J. Vanhoozer and Stanley E. Porter.

14. Vanhoozer, "Into the Great 'Beyond': A Theologian's Response to the Marshall Plan," in Marshall, *Beyond the Bible*, 81–95, especially 87.

matter, is again right: a besetting problem in evangelical accounts is their tendency to reduce doctrine to what the Bible *teaches*, with the concomitant focus on affirming what Bovell calls "propositional truths."

In line with Vanhoozer, and his cultural-linguistic precursor George Lindbeck,[15] I think the more focused and helpful question is: What practices is the doctrine of inspiration aimed at informing, shaping, and—in due course—reforming? How, in other words, does the inspiration of Scripture regulate Christian living and understanding?

A doctrinally oriented account of this matter will focus on how Scripture is put to work in God's economy for the purposes of drawing the Christian, *as reader of Scripture*, towards God. Where Chapman brings us to the point of seeing that Scripture is "entirely meaningful" in connection with expressing the will of God to its readers,[16] I think the difference a doctrinal approach makes is to relocate the focus away from being a reader, and towards being a Christian who is also a reader. This is an important, if subtle, distinction.

It might be brought out by juxtaposing two particularly perceptive observations made by David Law in his own treatment of the doctrine of inspiration. On the one hand, he responds to those who seek to reduce the significance of the doctrine on the grounds that there is nothing in the text to which it corresponds: this "is certainly right in [its] claim that there is no specific element in the text that we can identify as inspiration. But this is a trivial point, arising, in my opinion, from a failure to understand the nature, function and purpose of the concept of inspiration."[17] Inspiration, doctrinally speaking, is properly located under the rubric of divine action, in connection with Scripture, but with the emphasis on what God is accomplishing in and through it. Thus: "It is in their capacity to encourage self-transformation on the part of the reader that the inspired status of the biblical texts resides."[18]

Overall, Law offers an excellent review of traditional theories which seek to link the Bible with God, dividing them (most helpfully) into word-centered and non-verbal theories of inspiration. The former includes all

---

15. George A. Lindbeck, *The Nature of Doctrine: Religion and Theology in a Postliberal Age* (Philadelphia: Westminster, 1984).

16. Chapman, "Reclaiming Inspiration," 188.

17. David R. Law, *Inspiration of the Scriptures* (London and New York: Continuum, 2001), 139.

18. Law, *Inspiration of the Scriptures*, 190.

the usual conservative suspects: instrumental theories, dictation theories, verbal and plenary inspiration, and a brief rehearsal of the doctrine of inerrancy, along with its problems.[19] The latter takes in a range of instructive proposals which seek to locate inspiration in some aspect of Scripture other than straightforwardly in the words upon the page: Charles Gore on the Bible's moral and spiritual teachings; William Sanday on inspiration as being selected by God; Austin Farrer locating it in the *images* of the Bible (which is Law's choice for the most helpful theory in this regard); William Abraham seeing Scripture as an inspired teacher; and Paul Achtemeier offering a "social" theory of inspiration concerning the long-term processes by which Scripture came to be collected.[20] For Law, the way ahead is not to reject the doctrine of inspiration, though he does discuss this alternative, but to seek to rehabilitate it with an account of transcendence, indebted to Karl Jaspers. He develops a general view of what Jaspers calls "ciphers," which allow ongoing human access to the divine realm beyond normal existence. The result is an "existential" account which sees Scripture as proffering a range of key ciphers which facilitate access to the divine, hence his above definition of inspiration as relating to the encouragement of self-transformation.

In my view, one need not find his own constructive proposal entirely compelling in order to see the value of his survey of other approaches and careful delineation of their problems. Whether a more existentially-orientated account does enough justice to the complex balancing of human and divine action in and through Scripture is perhaps a question, although it is only fair to note that his book has something of the air of a manifesto rather than a fully worked-out account in terms of dealing with actual transformative encounters with particular texts.[21] Here, it will suffice to note that the direction of travel is simply different from that which Bovell joins in his attempt to broaden out a doctrine of inspiration. If one follows Law's kind of approach, one comes to Scripture alert for the theological dimensions of transformative encounter, which a doctrine of inspiration is seeking to safeguard, or, in some sense, to regulate. The commitment to persist with the reading and studying of Holy Scripture in life before God is surely right at the heart of a doctrine of its inspiration, and here, as in so much else,

---

19. Law, *Inspiration of the Scriptures*, 41–97.

20. Ibid., 99–135. In the process, Law reviews most of the key studies of the issue in the preceding century, such as those by the people named here.

21. Though this is a growing area in other aspects of biblical studies. For one recent practical example, see John Riches, et al., *What is Contextual Bible Study? A practical guide with group studies for Advent and Lent* (London: SPCK, 2010).

biblical scholars may profit from learning more the ways of theologians in order to attain to a more deeply Christian practice of engaging Scripture.[22]

Conclusion

I am, again, grateful to Carlos Bovell for his invitation to engage with what is a timely and suggestive attempt to think afresh with the notion of the inspiration of Scripture. I hope it will be clear that I think his affirmations about the role of the Spirit in the reader, and the concomitant bigger ("supplemented") picture of inspiration which he defends, have considerable merit on the terms within which he proposes them. In this response, I have sought to suggest that, in some respects, his remains a proposal that, having wrestled the demons of inerrancy in the night, has walked away with a pronounced limp. It is not that it does not offer an alternative—it does. But there is a doctrine of inspiration which may yet lift weary readers up on eagles' wings, and carry them towards a transforming encounter with God (the God of Jesus Christ, the God of Scripture. . .). Such a blessing, and on its own terms, is most eagerly to be sought.

---

22. Thus, for one powerful account, Stephen E. Fowl, *Engaging Scripture. A Model for Theological Interpretation* (Oxford: Blackwell, 1998).

An "Inspired" Theory of Truth and a Pluralism Worthy of God

Mark S. McLeod-Harrison

CARLOS BOVELL OPENS HIS essay with a quotation from Roger Nicole who said that the Bible is "God breathed, his word, of indefectible authority, clothed with God's own truthfulness" (3). In the context Bovell responds to, one assumption is that God's truthfulness has to do more-or-less with God communicating via propositions and little else. But that assumption doesn't note how ambiguous the phrase "God's own truthfulness" is. Of course, to be truthful includes the notion that one is telling the truth in words. But it also indicates telling the truth, say, with body language. But telling the truth is not merely about communicating accurate "content." Take, for instance, the claim that Yahweh is the true God. The true God, one presumes, is a contrast to all the other fake and posturing gods. "God's truthfulness" is protean and pregnant in meaning. God's character is truthful and that grounds truth-telling, but if God tells us the truth, it is because God is Truth and cannot merely be summed up by a list of truths.

When Bovell reacts against the proposition-only based understanding of inspiration, I have few, if any, quibbles. In fact, in my own work I've referred to, albeit indirectly, the sorts of hesitations Bovell has about understanding inspiration strictly propositionally. Bovell writes: "For evangelicals . . . much rides on a correct view of the inspiration and authority of the Bible, and for some believers, this includes their salvation" (6). In one of my past projects, I explicitly identified a sort of Christian believer who holds such a view, understanding that one's salvation depended upon "getting it right" in our theological descriptions, on pain of losing one's salvation if

An "Inspired" Theory of Truth and a Pluralism Worthy of God

one doesn't.[1] But that is not the view I hold, and consequently I have substantial sympathy with Bovell's essay.

As an alternative to criticism, I want to provide some philosophical support to Bovell's view. In particular, my concern is to describe, albeit with too much brevity, a theory of truth that helps to ground the sort of position Bovell proposes. I then want briefly to present an ontological structure that not only allows but embraces the pluralism about interpretive positions found among readers of the Christian Scriptures. I have explicated and defended both views elsewhere but they have not been applied directly to the context of a doctrine of inspiration.[2]

If Scripture is alive, as Bovell claims, with the vitality of God, it is helpful to be able to spell out how truth—and what kind of truth—is communicated through such vitality. In particular, I have in mind the nature of the truth-value bearers via which God's revelation is communicated. Bovell writes that ". . . both human beings and the Scriptures are portrayed as God-breathed, with the implication that by virtue of possessing God's spirit—by virtue of God's creative act of breathing life into them—the two respective entities, humans and Scripture, are thought to be in possession of God's very 'life,' his 'vitality'" (7). The very life of God is in us and in Scripture. Thus, God's very truthfulness is available to us via the Scriptures. But what, exactly, is truth? In addition, I want to explore some potential implications built into Bovell's approach. In particular, I'm thinking of what it means to say that God has life. What does that mean in the context of a relationship between a text, a reader, other people, and God's own personhood? Is there room here for a more pluralistic approach to God's own nature, and theology more generally, that goes beyond mere epistemological disagreements?

I

Let us begin with the theory of truth. It has long been a value of evangelical theology to understand truth as a type of correspondence between beliefs and reality. Correspondence theories of truth, however, raise a host of issues. One of the most problematic was noticed over 100 years ago by G. Frege who remarked that correspondence is a relation between two things. But for two things to correspond perfectly, we would be dealing with a

---

1. See my *Repairing Eden* (Montreal: McGill-Queens University Press, 2005).

2. See my *Make/Believing the World(s): Toward a Christian Ontological Pluralism* (Montreal: McGill-Queen's University Press, 2009) for details.

single thing rather than two distinct things. This would mean that truth requires identity between the truth-value bearer and the truth maker, which is a definition of truth that none of us use in practice.³ Perhaps we can get around such problems, if they are really problems (a view I reject below), by noting that behind correspondence theories is what can be thought of as a minimalist but realistic theory of truth. A minimalist realist theory of truth could be fleshed out via correspondence but need not be. We can say that a minimalist realist theory of truth is committed to little more than this where p denotes a proposition: "p" is true if and only if p. As William Alston proposes, a realist theory of truth of a minimalist type says that when "p" is true, the world is the way "p" says it is.⁴ Here we have, apparently, two things: "p" and the way the world is. That is, we have a truth-value bearer and a truth maker. But how do what *appear* to be two things go together to make for truth?

We can start with the fairly standard reply that "p" is a belief. Beliefs, however, suffer from an ambiguity sometimes called the "act/object" ambiguity. That is, beliefs are both mental attitudes (a sort of action, we might say) and the content of the belief (its object). Standardly, then, what is proposed is that the object-belief is either true or false, and not the act-belief. The object-belief is the putative content. Upon further analysis, it is standardly proposed that object-beliefs are propositions.⁵ It is, thus, propositions that are said to be true or false. Evangelical theology has often been right in line with these philosophical points. In order to avoid the perceived fears of experience-based or neo-orthodox versions of inspiration, evangelicals have often held fast to propositions as objective entities made true (when they are) by objective facts. This is taken to avoid the supposedly subjective results of experiential accounts of inspiration. The emphasis is thus on the term "objective." Evangelicals have often feared the potential relativity of experience or of giving too much credence to the role of the human interpreter.

---

3. See G. Frege, "The Thought," reprinted in *Philosophical Logic*, ed. P. Strawson (New York: Oxford University Press, 1967), 17–38.

4. See William P. Alston, *A Realist Conception of Truth* (Ithaca, NY: Cornell University Press, 1996).

5. There are other possibilities here as well, including assertions, statements, utterances, and sentences (either token or type). I'm not considering these alternatives here but have taken them up in detail elsewhere. See *Make/Believing the World(s)*, especially chapter 9.

Hence Bovell's countermove: "My contention is that precisely those two facets of spiritual activity are what properly constitute biblical inspiration. The first is *the words of Scripture*, in whatever form they take throughout the long process of their growth, transmission, and reception. The second is *the hermeneutical matrix provided for Scripture by readers of Scripture*—but not just *any* readers: only readers who *possess the Spirit*, the Spirit of Life that would be given to them *after* Christ has been 'glorified'" (8).

I take it to be an important assumption behind this two-aspect approach to inspiration that propositions are not, strictly speaking, mental. Nevertheless, truths are the kinds of things people know, hold, or believe and hence a clear role exists for the mental. What has to be explained, then, is the relationship between our mental access to propositions and the propositions themselves, as well as the relationship of propositions to the world. Recall Frege's argument about the correspondence theory, viz., that the two things (in our case, proposition and world) must be identical if there is to be total correspondence. His view (which he later rejected for the position that truth could not be defined) has come to be called the identity theory of truth. Propositions, it is argued, are just facts.[6] This view explains the relationship of the (true) proposition and the world, viz., identity. But it doesn't capture how the proposition is related to the mental on account of a radical idealism where the proposition itself is a mental entity and the world swallowed up in human thought. But *where*, so to speak, are propositions? Do they, as Alvin Plantinga once asked, "exist in serene and majestic independence of persons and their means of apprehension?"[7] Plantinga argues that they exist in the mind of God. But is that enough? Yes, though only for *necessary* truths that have always existed in the mind of God. But what about *contingent* truths, including the fact that God created a world in which human persons exist and are fundamentally able to interact with the divine self?

Here's where the twin doctrines of revelation and inspiration come into play. How do we humans access the mind of God or, short of that, propositions about God? If Frege's argument is correct, and we want to hold fast to a realist account of truth, it seems that the identity theory of truth is right: "p" is true if and only if p, where the proposition "p" and an aspect of the world (p) are identical. Do the propositions and the facts of the world

---

6. Philosophers Michael Lynch, Jennifer Hornsby, and John McDowell (albeit under a different description) defend this view.

7. Alvin Plantinga, "How to be an Anti-realist," *Proceedings and Addresses of the American Philosophical Association* 56 (1982): 66–67.

exist in God's mind? Well, yes. But how should we think about human access to those truths?

Here, I want to return to the distinction between the act-belief and the object-belief. Object-beliefs, at least the true ones, are identical to bits of the world. So far, however, we have little access to them. But what if, contrary to much contemporary theory of truth, it isn't object-beliefs that are truth-value bearers but rather act-beliefs? That is, what if what is true (or false) is the propositional attitude of belief rather than the content of belief—the proposition? We can call this the worldly content theory of truth (or WCT). Briefly stated, it says:

> WCT: For all x, x is a true (act-)belief if and only if the content of x is actually in x.

Or stated differently:

> WCT*: For all x, x is a true (act-)belief if and only if the content of x is (part of) the world.

The phrase "actually in" in WCT is meant to emphasize that it is the act-belief that is in touch with some aspect of the actual world and thus it is the act-belief (rather than its content) that is true. WCT says the same thing as WCT* because to be actually in a person's act-belief is simply for the appropriate chunk of the world to be the content of a person's act-belief.

The obvious challenge here, and something behind a good deal of evangelical worry about non-correspondence theories of truth, is the fear that we humans somehow "make-up" the truth—the specter of radical idealism. That is a result, potentially, of epistemic (and perhaps pragmatic) theories of truth, theories where truth is determined by the "grand scientific research project." But it is important to see that we aren't making up the truth on WCT. Truth is objectively rooted not in our epistemologies, but in the way the world is. WCT is, in short, a realist theory of truth quite compatible with the minimalist account proposed by Alston. Other concerns with non-correspondence theories such as deflationary or coherence theories are that truth either is not a real property (deflationary theories) or that it is relative (coherence theories). WCT is, again, a realist theory so that truth is a real property (attached to an act-belief, when true). Although WCT is consistent with an ontological pluralism, it is not necessarily committed to pluralism.[8] The advantage of such an account for Bovell's theory of inspiration

---

8. It is important to see, however, that WCT is compatible with ontological pluralisms of a variety of sorts. See *Make/Believing the World(s)* for a detailed and extended

is that it unites the two features he is concerned to preserve: the words of the text and the spirit-filled reader/interpreter. The theory opens the door for God's expression of the divine being in something other than propositions (understood as detached, free-standing claims). The very liveliness of the inspired text—its vitality—is the very Spirit of God. It is God who is revealed via the inspired text and not merely propositions about God.

The God of the Bible is the God who reveals. But what does God reveal? Propositions? Well, yes. But surely what evangelicals want is not merely a list of true propositions about God and divine interaction with humans in history. What we want is a relationship with the very God who loves us. Here we come to the importance of Bovell's analogy between his view of inspiration and the life of prayer. It is not just true propositions about God (one step, on a non-identity theory of truth, removed from God) but God's own glorious, loving, and gracious person who is present to our minds when we have true act-beliefs. Thus Bovell: "Both Scripture and human beings are each made alive by being separately infused with God's spirit, but they are also *coordinately enlivened in relation to one another* by virtue of what I propose to call 'biblical inspiration'" (12). Here it is worth recalling something Colin Gunton wrote:

> Human being in the image of God is to be understood relationally rather than in terms of the possession of fixed characteristics such as reason or will, as has been the almost universal tendency of the [Western, Christian] tradition. By this I mean that the reality of the human creature must be understood in terms of the human relation to God, in the first instance, and to the rest of creation in the second. The relation to the remainder of creation falls into two. In the first place, to be in the image of God is to subsist in relations of mutual constitutiveness with other human beings. In the second place, it is to be in a set of relations with the non-personal creation. The human imaging of God is a dynamic way of being before God and with the fellow creature.[9]

God is more fundamentally a relational being than a being best described by propositions, true or not. It is the God who loves us, who creates us as social beings to be recipients of that love, and who reveals the divine love via the inspired Scriptures. But surely God cannot do that without

---

defense of this claim.

9. Colin Gunton, *The One, the Three, and the Many* (New York: Cambridge University Press, 1993), 3.

socially involving us in the process. Hence comes to the fore the importance of Bovell's push toward realigning the doctrines of inspiration and illumination.

But at this point, more challenges to the correspondence theory of truth come forward. If we let God be God (that is, be fully who God is) and yet we are to grasp God's reality, won't we be ever distant and removed from God's very reality? In other words, won't we always be falling short of God and, thereby, forever stuck in an epistemological quagmire? Here I think another one of Bovell's comments needs to be explored. In evaluating the typical doctrine of illumination promoted by evangelicals, he notes the following:

> Another reservation that I have with the teacher model of illumination has to do with how the Holy Spirit has putatively taught different churches throughout history different propositions that cannot all be accepted without contradiction. Some Christians may seek to get around this objection by affirming that he has taught the doctrines found in *their own* church's statement of faith while at the same time denying that the Holy Spirit has taught the doctrines found in *other* churches' statements of faith. Such a position, however, seems a little too convenient to take seriously (18).

The problem here appears to be the emphasis on propositions along with an evangelical fear of ontological pluralism. Perhaps if there were no propositions about God revealed through the inspired text of the Bible, then the problem of theological pluralism would disappear. But Bovell is not denying the existence of true propositions about God. There are both words *and* readers involved in the inspirational process. How then to affirm the plural understandings of God without losing God entirely in mystery?

II

Earlier I noted that the worldly content theory of truth does not imply, but is compatible with, ontological pluralism. I will now say something about that compatibility. The worldly content theory of truth provides a framework for explaining the extensive pluralism found among theological claims without losing the objectivity of God. Yet I am not only proposing that WCT is compatible with an ontological pluralism about the created world but, furthermore, that the pluralism extends to God's very being. Humans use conceptual schemes to shape the world into the things that are. But they

An "Inspired" Theory of Truth and a Pluralism Worthy of God

are not all the same. And so, since there are competing conceptual schemes, there are competing ways things are, extending from scientific entities all the way to theological realities—which is not to say there are no limits on the various ways the world is. Limits are in place because God puts them there. But even God is different ways in different conceptual schemes. In conjunction with the enlivened text of Scripture (the presence of the Holy Spirit therein), we enlivened humans create the ways the world is. We can call this ontological view, "theistic irrealism."

What are some details? A theory of truth—at least a realist one—does not tell us anything about how the world gets to be the way it is. Christians are committed to the view that God creates and sustains the world. But how God does those things is far more open to theorizing than is often thought by Christian philosophers and theologians. Theistic irrealism is, in broad outline, the view that God creates the *Urstoff* of the world but allows, and in fact encourages, humans to make and shape the preliminary "stuff" into the way(s) the world is. Humans are made in God's image and one fundamental way in which that image is exemplified is through human creativity. While typically Christians think that the world came into being shaped very much the way in which we experience it, it is plausible to think that the reason our experience of the world "matches" the world so well is that our very thoughts, ideas, concepts, and so forth shape the raw material created by God into the way the world is. Stated in other terms, the conceptual schemes found quite diversely among humans actually make the world the various ways it is.

The proposal before us is a proposal for pluralism yet it is no mere epistemological relativism but deeply ontological. In other words, it is not providing for merely Lockean nominalist essences but rather essences that make the world the way(s) it actually is. There are many conceptual schemes, and hence, many actual ways the world is. It is a theistically rooted, relativized Kantianism.[10] A host of questions will need to be answered about this account.[11] Two of the most pressing are: how might this work and doesn't it simply lead to contradictions? In explaining how the theory works, it should become plain how the problem of contradictions is to be handled.[12]

---

10. Substantial aspects of this proposal find their roots in the work of Nelson Goodman and Michael Lynch. See *Make/Believing the World(s)* for details.

11. Here again, I refer the interested reader to my book, *Make/Believing the World(s)*.

12 For a fuller treatment, see *Make/Believing the Word(s)*.

First, we must distinguish between necessities and contingencies. God holds the former (such as mathematical and logical truths and God's own necessary existence) in the divine being. These are truths that hold across all human conceptual schemes. That is, there is no way a mere human (or even a large group of humans) is responsible for the fact that 2 + 2 = 4. That is a truth that holds no matter what conceptual scheme humans contrive. Typically, such truths are thought of as absolutes, where the notion of absolute is thought of as *propositions true, independent of all conceptual schemes*. Michael Lynch notes the fact, typically overlooked, that *absolutes need not be independent of all conceptual schemes but could simply be true in every conceptual scheme*.[13] Lynch calls these "virtual absolutes" to contrast them with the typical way in which absolutes are understood. All necessities are virtual absolutes according to theistic irrealism. From a Christian point of view, it is important to note that, so far as necessities go, God too has a conceptual scheme and because God is, so to speak, "in the mix" with us in creating the world in which we live, God's creative consistency supports necessities as they turn up in the contingent order. Humans, in other words, do not create the necessities, whether mathematical laws or God.

Contingencies are more complicated. The created order in which we live is not necessary. However, it is initially created, shaped, and influenced in substantial ways by God. Christians *qua* Christians would be unorthodox to think otherwise. I am proposing that *the details of how the world is* are largely up to us. As postmodern theorists sometimes say, it appears that the world is many different ways and those ways contradict one another. The mistake of the more radically postmodern among us is their claim that there is no meta-narrative. For Christians (and if Christianity is true, for everyone), there is a meta-narrative, viz., the story of the work of God in creation and redemption—the work of God among us. But that meta-narrative is not the whole story. There are many ways the world is, even though there is a meta-narrative.

Theistic irrealism proposes that we think of the Christian meta-narrative in terms of thin properties. Let's start with God. God is omniscient, omnipotent, omnipresent, and omnibenevolent. But let us think of these divine properties as thin properties. That is, when two theologians are discussing God, they will both agree that God has those properties and that they are speaking of the same things, viz., God and the divine properties; however, those same two theologians might understand God and

---

13. See Michael P. Lynch, *Truth in Context* (Cambridge, MA.: MIT Press, 1998).

the divine properties quite differently. That is, in the conceptual schemes they use, they "thicken" up the properties of omniscience, omnipotence, omnipresence, and omnibenevolence quite differently, perhaps even in contradictory ways. Theistic irrealism holds that when the claims are taken out of the context of their conceptual schemes (or put in a possible world in which the claims were relative to the same scheme), they would be logically inconsistent. It's just that we do not live in a world where the claims can be taken out of the context of their conceptual schemes. So there is real inconsistency, but it is not a real problem. There are many ways God is (so far as God allows the divine self to interact with human creativity) in the world that God has created.[14]

Let us consider in more detail how the meta-narrative works by supposing that the Nicene Creed summarizes orthodox Christian thought. The Creed can be understood as applying thin properties to God and God's relationship to the world. Those thin properties, however, can be thickened up in a variety of ways and some of those ways conflict (when taken out of the context of their conceptual schemes). So Christ died for sinners, but there are many true (and conflicting) ways the atonement works. For example, both the substitutionary view of the atonement and the moral view of the atonement are true. Yet they are contradictory to one another and because they *are* contradictory, the world is plural ways. This is possible precisely because God encourages humans to shape, via their conceptual schemes, the many ways the world is.

On the level of thin concepts, one can see how God's existence and the core nature of God are preserved across all conceptual schemes. On the level of thick concepts, however, God might be quite different in different theological conceptual schemes. This is no mere epistemological difference but true ontological difference. God is one way in conceptual scheme A and God is another (conflicting) way in conceptual scheme B. But at the divine core, God is not dependent upon human conceptual schemes at all (although logically dependent on the divine conceptual scheme). Here, there is plenty of room for the mystery of God and for a significant human role found in Bovell's version of inspiration.

God is not contingent, but the world in which we live is. If God had not created it, there would be no such world. Humans, according to theistic

---

14. It is important to remember that God is a necessity and therefore God's thin properties "turn up" in every conceptual scheme. The same need not be true of contingent things and their thin properties.

irrealism, play a central role in that world. Indeed, we make the world in substantial ways. But humans are not necessities. However, once made, humans contribute in significant ways to the way the world is, beyond just changing things within their "designed and fixed" categories. That is, humans don't just make houses out of trees but humans make the trees themselves! (Conceptually, of course.) Consider, for example, that what counts as a tree in Saskatchewan would often merely count as a large shrub in British Columbia, or consider that the number of things in a bag changes depending what you mean by the word "thing"—do you include only material objects or relationships among them as well? There are limits, however, on what humans can do with their creativity. Humans cannot, first off, make the *Urstoff*. Furthermore, humans cannot conceptualize God into nonexistence (because God is a necessary being). Nor can they conceptualize each other into nonexistence (not because humans are necessary, but because God sustains us). We can try to wallpaper over God and other people, but we will not find success. Such conceptual schemes, in the end, collapse into themselves. God's existence is necessary and human existence, given God's creative work, is central to there being the world in which we live and the various ways it is. If we wallpaper over God or humans, we lose morality but also the creative source of the world along with the world itself.

It is important to recognize how major a component eschatology is for theistic irrealism. God is in the mix with us. God is providential in the divine interaction with human persons and the rest of the created order. All of our conceptual schemes are partially, incompletely, and wrongly constructed. By this, I don't mean that they fall short of "the" truth, but that they are not "rightly rendered" (as Nelson Goodman suggests). But God, who superintends the working and ordering of the world, will bless some conceptual schemes and not bless others. Or at least, God will require some substantial editing work of us when God is fully revealed. Here, it is important to note that there will never be a "single, true description" of God that is revealed. Rather, the full revelation of God is the revelation of God's own self, which would include a fuller revelation of God's commitment to human creativity. There will not be a revelation of a singular, true set of propositions about God. In heaven, God will still be many ways, as will the heavenly frameworks in which we will live. God's self-revelation will still occur within our conceptual frameworks. It's just that those frameworks will be more fully developed—more nearly rightly rendered.

An "Inspired" Theory of Truth and a Pluralism Worthy of God

The basic proposal of theistic irrealism is applicable to many areas of academic study: the physical sciences, the human sciences, and the arts and literature (recall the various paradigms discussed by Kuhn).[15] Competing, and apparently equally viable and conflicting, theories and pictures are present in each of these domains. Could it be that they (or at least many of them) are true or well-made? I believe the answer is a resounding "yes!" And that is the case even though they conflict one with another. Thus, the pluralism noted by Bovell has a good explanation and is, indeed, itself a good thing. God is plural ways and each of those ways, when well-formed by human conceptual schemes, describes God truly. Those truths are not undermined by being contradictory across schemes. Rather, the richness that is the God of the Scriptures is highlighted and celebrated by the theological diversity found not only in the Scripture itself, but also in the many various and quite different theologies that abound.[16]

In the end, however, the most important thing about the combination of WCT and theistic irrealism is that it allows for something more than propositional knowledge. It allows for personal knowledge, relational knowledge, knowledge rooted in the social world. Gunton notes that "to be in the image of God is to subsist in relations of mutual constitutiveness with other human beings." I think we can take this one step further. To be in the image of God is to be inspired by God, to be vivified in the divine life. We thus interact with and are molded by God's own being—Truth itself. But this Truth is not merely propositional information but Reality itself. We are constituted by God, at least so far as we exist within God's creative purview. But does God exist in this same ontological space and is God therefore (partly) constituted by us? I believe so. The inspirational circle comes full circle. If that is correct, not only is inspiration of the text accounted for via the life of God, but we believers actually contribute to the life of God.

---

15. See Thomas Kuhn, *The Structure of Scientific Revolutions* (3rd ed.; Chicago: University of Chicago Press, 1996).

16. I refer the interested reader to *Make/Believing the World(s)* for more details on how to understand the ontological pluralism merely pointed to in the last few paragraphs.

The Authority of Scripture

The External Authority of Scripture

Carlos R. Bovell

IF THE SCRIPTURES ARE "hermeneutically God-breathed" as I proposed above, it might be asked, "With what authority are they vested for contemporary believers?" If Bible readers play such an integral role in the Bible's "inspiration" (on account of both the Scriptures' and believers' possessing the same Spirit), does that mean its *readers* ultimately legitimate the authority of Scripture? Or put another way, am I effectively transferring the Bible's objective authority *from* the Bible as God's Word *to* the readers' subjective authority as interpreters (in their capacity as God's people)?

In this chapter, I will offer some thoughts on what kind of "external" authority Scripture might be said to have. In the next, I will consider what "internal" authority Scripture might be said to possess. In both of these chapters, I will be departing from traditional evangelical views on the authority of Scripture by taking seriously the observation that it is the hermeneutical role of the Bible's believing readers that at least partly confers authority on Scripture, both "internally" and "externally."

R. Bauckham describes "external" authority as a case in which a given statement, command, or prescription is accepted because the person making it is deemed qualified to do so. He describes "internal" authority as a case where a statement made, command issued, or prescription offered convinces a person on its own merits. In this case, the authority of the person making the statement is not at issue because the merits of the statement itself demand assent.[1] For present purposes, I propose that the core of the New Testament's "external" authority is grounded in the fact that the earliest NT books contain traditions and teachings that grew out of the experience of believers who saw God when the risen Jesus appeared to them by the power of the Holy Spirit.

---

1. See R. Bauckham, "Scripture and Authority," *Transformation* 15 (1998): 5–6.

The Authority of Scripture

1. Authority as Partially Conferred on Scripture by Readers

Generally speaking, evangelicals are not comfortable with the idea that readers of the NT are a fundamental part of the process of inspiring holy Scripture and, as such, play an active role in giving it its authority. Traditionally, there has not been room for the role of *readers* in evangelical doctrines of Scripture. Even those that putatively acknowledge a role for the community's involvement in establishing the canon would balk at the assertion that the Bible's readers make real and substantive contributions to inspiring Scripture, much less endowing it with authority.[2]

For example, in a recent article T. Löfstedt reflects upon how evangelicals might respond to common criticisms of "sola scriptura."[3] During the course of his discussion, Löfstedt raises a number of very important questions regarding the relationship between the church universal, the apostles, and the NT texts. His overall aim is to defend why the NT texts should always be given priority when compared to any other form of "tradition." Throughout the essay, Löfstedt offers wise counsel, helpfully pointing out that the primary reason the NT texts retain authority for Christians today is because "the present NT canon contains the best witnesses available to the life and teaching of Jesus and the apostles" (66). Although he makes a good start, what I find lacking in Löfstedt's article is a concomitant emphasis on the textual, paratextual, and hermeneutical roles that the NT's readers necessarily play for both *establishing and re-establishing* the authority of Scripture throughout Christian history.[4]

That the source of biblical authority extends beyond a simple appeal to canon is made clear by any reading of church history. All positions, not

---

2. M. Kruger, for example, superimposes an artificial, trinitarian perichoresis over three of the main scholarly proposals of the NT canon, conveniently sidestepping all textual, paratextual and hermeneutical dynamics that readers introduce. M. Kruger, *Canon Revisited: Establishing the Origins and Authority of the New Testament Books* (Wheaton, IL: Crossway, 2012).

3. "In Defence of the Scripture Principle: An Evangelical Reply to A. S. Khomiakov," *Evangelical Quarterly* 83 (2011): 49–72.

4. For a study of the textual and paratextual issues surrounding Paul's letters, for example, see E. Scherbenske, *Canonizing Paul: Ancient Editorial Practice and the Corpus Paulinum* (New York: Oxford University Press, 2013). In *Gospel Writing: A Canonical Perspective* (Grand Rapids: Eerdmans, 2013), F. Watson draws attention to the "often obscure distinctions between inscription, interpretation, and reinterpretation" of the Gospel materials (357).

just my own, must reckon with the active contribution of the Bible's readers when accounting for biblical authority. Even a more restrictive construal of biblical *inspiration*—like one that confines divine inspiration to texts and/or authors—has to explain why Christianity has always been typified by a thoroughgoing pluralism. As Vogels observes, "The problem of pluralism in unity exists as well in the community which produced the Bible as in the community which reads it."[5] Even those traditions that pride themselves on their strict adherence to biblicism could not stem the tide of interpretive pluralism within their ranks.[6] Pluralism is now so widespread that Löfstedt feels a need to apologize for it in his paper. He writes:

> Some 160 years have gone by since Khomiakov penned his critique of the Western confessions, and there are more Protestant denominations now than there were then. But in many respects divisions between Evangelical Protestants are less significant now than they were when Khomiakov wrote his articles. Evangelical Protestants read each others' books, study at each others' seminaries, support each others' ministries, and readily move from one denomination to another.[7]

What Löfstedt appears to be saying is that interpretive and doctrinal pluralism have now become such a normal part of contemporary evangelical culture that it no longer troubles anyone. The question arises, however, whether a thoroughgoing pluralism *should* trouble anyone. That is, given popular evangelical bibliological suppositions regarding Scripture's unerring authority, shouldn't evangelicals see thoroughgoing pluralism within Evangelicalism as a problem?[8]

---

5. W. Vogels, "Three Possible Modes of Inspiration," in *Scrittura Ispirata: Atti del Simposio internazionale sull'ispirazione promosso dall'Ateneo Pontificio "Regina Apostolorum,"* ed. A. Izquierdo (Citta del Vaticano: Libreria Editrice Vaticana 2002), 77.

6. C. Smith explores this topic in his monograph on evangelical "biblicism." See Smith, *The Bible Made Impossible: Why Biblicism Is Not a Truly Evangelical Reading of Scripture* (Grand Rapids: Brazos, 2012).

7. Löfstedt, "Defence," 71.

8. The pluralism is so great that many writers have even questioned whether the designation "evangelical" reveals anything meaningful.

2. Scripture Is Authoritative Because It Helps Direct People to Christ

Either way, an important difference between my approach to inspiration and that of more conservative evangelicals is that, whereas I am open to having interpretive pluralism feature prominently in an evangelical account of Scripture's authority, biblicists see nothing wrong with carrying on *as though the pluralism did not exist*.[9] Remarking on one of the implicit aims of the Chicago Statement of Inerrancy, for example, A. Vos keenly observes: "One sure way to eliminate bad interpretation is to eliminate all interpretation, and at certain points this is what the inerrancist is trying to do."[10]

On my account, by contrast, there is a ready answer for why a full-blown pluralism *should* characterize historic Christianity. To wit, interpretive pluralism is precisely what one will *expect* because the very process of inspiring the Bible is intrinsically tied to the spiritual, hermeneutical activity of the interpreters themselves. This means that the inspiration of the Bible is a dynamic, ongoing process that is never discursively finished. Indeed, the inspiration of Scripture, which includes readers just as much as it does the biblical tradents (and texts), is continuing and will continue throughout the history of Christ's churches, i.e., throughout the time period when human beings can be pointed to Christ.

As W. Kirchschläger explains, "In reading the Bible, a person encounters the same divine spirit that stands behind the writing down of the word of God. This means that inspiration covers not only the process of writing but also the process of receiving, of reading the Bible. God pronounces His word throughout the generations to those who are willing to face it in the Scriptures."[11] Far from undermining Scripture's authority, various churches' hermeneutical engagement with the Bible is precisely what makes it possible for the Bible to remain "alive and active" throughout the ages. This ongoing hermeneutical-spiritual process whereby Scripture's

---

9. When plurality is brought to their attention, evangelical theologians and philosophers like to minimize its scope by emphasizing that all evangelicals hold certain core doctrines in common, but as Smith observes, "Most evangelicals will of course affirm together that Jesus died on the cross to save people from sin. But scratch just below the surface, and disagreement emerges." See C. Smith, *Bible Made Impossible*, 188.

10. Vos, "Infallible of Inerrant? The Scope of the Bible's Message," *Reformed Journal* 30.5 (1980): 20.

11. See Kirchschläger, "Scripture and Inspiration," in *Understanding Scripture: Explorations of Jewish and Christian Traditions of Interpretation*, ed. C. Thoma and M. Wyschogrod (Mahwah, NJ: Paulist, 1987), 43.

readers continue the activity of inspiration is what qualifies Scripture as authoritative for believers. By directing people to the person of Jesus Christ, Scripture has always been and will always remain an integral component of all Christian living and community, a component that Christians should never think they can faithfully live without.

Perhaps this helps explain why many inerrantist evangelicals are so uncomfortable with the history of biblical interpretation: they are made to feel awkward by the sheer discontinuity one encounters in both Christian thought and practice. The pluralism that obtains throughout the history of the churches' interaction with Scripture, in the many ways that Scripture has been directing people to Christ, can pose an inherent challenge to faith for many evangelical students. As Berger and Luckmann famously noted, "Pluralism encourages both skepticism and innovation and is thus inherently subversive of the taken-for-granted reality of the traditional *status quo*."[12] Perhaps this partially accounts too for the serious disconnection between contemporary evangelical understandings of the history of the doctrine of Scripture and the way exegetes actually approached Scripture throughout the first 1500 years of the history of Christianity. On the whole, evangelicals have been slow to appreciate just how indebted *sola scriptura* is to broader cultural developments in the Renaissance and Enlightenment.[13] They are right to gather that the main purpose of the Scriptures is to direct people to Christ. However, they err in thinking that Scripture's believing readers are not intrinsically and actively involved with endowing Scripture with its authority.

3. Readers Confer Authority on Scripture by Directing It to Christ via "Allegory"

Even more important for evangelical appropriations of *sola scriptura* than the advent of the Enlightenment are theological developments that took place during the early twentieth century. At this time, scholars at Old Princeton were deliberately constructing a distinctly apologetic approach

---

12. P. Berger and T. Luckmann, *The Social Construction of Reality: A Treatise in the Sociology of Knowledge* (Garden City, NY: Doubleday, 1966), 125.

13. Compare A. Louth who describes the *sola scriptura* principle as an "alliance between the Reformation and the Enlightenment." I suggest one way that the *sola scriptura* principle fit into its wider cultural context in *By Good and Necessary Consequence: A Preliminary Genealogy of Biblicist Foundationalism* (Eugene, OR: Wipf and Stock, 2009).

to Scripture that spoke to the fears latent in Protestant American culture-at-large. Old Princeton's apologetic was largely a response to the dual threats of the Graf-Wellhausen hypothesis and the new evolutionary approaches being introduced in the study of religion, which included the study of the Bible.[14] Over time, the Old Princeton strategy of defending the Bible became such an integral part of the broader, conservative Protestant culture that even today not a few (American) evangelicals understand their very Christian identity in light of the belief that their position on inerrancy is exactly the one held throughout historic Christianity.[15]

Even so, its adherents could only hold such an historical-theological claim to be true with considerable qualification. An important point that inerrantists downplay is just how integral the method of allegory is to the early churches' understanding of Scripture. *If evangelicals are going to attribute some form of "inerrancy" to the Church Fathers, they must make it compatible with the fact that ancient readers would resolve any embarrassing, unintelligible, or problematic passage in the Bible by reading it figuratively.* Frequent recourse to allegory (or typology) is what allowed Bible readers in ages past to escape the exegetical burden of having to apologize for infelicities they found in the biblical texts. Wherever necessary, ancient teachers of Scripture had no qualms about looking past "literal" readings and focusing on finding "spiritual" meanings that every Scripture was presumed to contain.[16] Gregory of Nyssa, to take one example, could think of at least four reasons for genuinely rejecting a literal reading of Scripture: "theological impropriety, physical or logical impossibility, uselessness, and immorality of the letter."[17]

Although allegorical/typological interpretation would take different forms for different readers, the hermeneutical outlook associated with figurative reading is not altogether different from the aim of contemporary evangelicals who read Scripture today. As Vos points out, nearly all evangelical parties agree that the right way to read the Bible is to try to establish for one's community what divine message it providentially conveys to them.

---

14. For an earlier discussion of these points, see Bovell, *Rehabilitating Inerrancy*, 118–21.

15. Warfield famously argued that the position he defended was both that of historic Christianity and that of the NT writers.

16. Compare D. H. Williams, *Evangelicals and Tradition: The Formative Influence of the Early Church* (Grand Rapids: Baker, 2005), 104.

17. R. Heine, "Gregory of Nyssa's Apology for Allegory," *Vigiliae Christianae* 38 (1984): 360.

At the same time, it is important *not* to settle prematurely for a culturally relative "human form" that God's message happens to be couched in.[18] The hermeneutical problem of distinguishing Scripture's "message" from its "medium" is one bequeathed to modern readers from the great socio-religious debates of antiquity.[19] For example, the problem of deciding what rites to maintain and which to treat spiritually dates at least as far back as the time of the ancient Pythagoreans (possibly fifth century BCE).[20] The rites that they thought should be kept were taken literally while those that could be done away with were taken figuratively.[21] The task was to uncover what deeper, spiritual truth they might contain. Rules for when and how to read Scripture figuratively have never been easy to delineate. Even Origen (185–254 CE), often dismissed as a hopeless allegorist,[22] accused some of *his* contemporaries of allegorizing Scripture without restraint.[23] Before him, the Jewish philosopher-cum-exegete Philo of Alexandria (ca. 20 BCE–40 CE) had registered similar complaints.[24]

Either way, it is hard to miss allegory's ministerial emphasis of deliberately connecting the message of Scripture to the spiritual demands of specific interpretive communities. J. Trigg draws attention to the pastoral concerns that informed the way Christian teachers interpreted Scripture in antiquity: "However sophisticated hermeneutically the Fathers were,

18. Vos, "Infallible?," 22.

19. In other words, there is no reason to make it into a *theological* problem.

20. K. Berthelot, "Philo and the Allegorical Interpretation of Homer in the Platonic Tradition (with an Emphasis on Porphyry's *De Antro Nympharum*)," in *Homer and the Bible in the Eyes of Ancient Interpreters*, ed. M. Niehoff (Boston: Brill, 2012), 168.

21. For the development of biblical laws for facilitating the divine-human encounter, see J. Kugel, "Some Unanticipated Consequences of the Sinai Revelation: A Religion of Laws," in *The Significance of Sinai : Traditions about Sinai and Divine Revelation in Judaism and Christianity*, ed. G. Brooke, H. Najman, and L. Stuckenbruck (New York: Brill, 2008), 1–13.

22. For example, Scalise writes that Origen, by following his proposed exegetical method, "demonstrates a loss of hermeneutical control." C. Scalise, "Allegorical Flights of Fancy: The Problem of Origen's Exegesis," *Greek Orthodox Theological Review* 32 (1987): 71

23. I. Ramelli, "The Philosophical Stance of Allegory in Stoicism and Its Reception in Platonism, Pagan and Christian: Origen in Dialogue with the Stoics and Plato," *International Journal of the Classical Tradition* 18 (2011): 335–71.

24. Long insists that the pattern for Philo's allegoresis is not to be found in Stoicism but in Heraclitus, whose approach became known to the Jewish predecessors that Philo himself mentions. See A. A. Long, "Allegory in Philo and Etymology in Stoicism: A Plea for Drawing Distinctions," *Studia Philonica Annual* 9 (1997): 198–210.

they could not conceive of interpreting the Bible in any way divorced of the needs of Christian community."[25] The ultimate goal of biblical exegesis in antiquity was to make Christ known from *both* Testaments of Scripture. The early church often called upon allegory to accomplish this. When and how this could be done would differ from teacher to teacher.

For example, Origen centered his allegoresis on the reality of the *incarnation*.[26] By contrast, Clement of Alexandria took Jesus' *crucifixion* as his starting point.[27] Meanwhile Augustine, who always tried to make sure that his approach to allegoresis was as principled as possible, concluded that *love of God and love of neighbor* should always be the goal of every teacher's exegesis.[28] H. Mayer's observation bears repeating: "If we were to decide the best method [of interpreting the Bible] by counting the number of Christian teachers and leaders in all ages who have practiced it, the allegorical method would win hands down."[29]

Notwithstanding, inerrantist evangelicals today tend to downplay the significance of allegory for the history of biblical interpretation. Inerrantist evangelicals who admit the points I have just made immediately discount them; they would prefer that the emphasis be placed on cases where the Scriptures are being treated "historically." In fact, they even argue that historical-literal readings were always used wherever possible.[30] The point to grasp, however, is that the early application of allegory to scriptural texts cannot indicate that the early churches had a "low" view of Scripture, as if owning up to the prevalence of figural readings in antiquity would diminish the early churches' esteem of the biblical texts. On the contrary, it was

---

25. Trigg, *Biblical Interpretation* (Wilmington, DE: Michael Glazier, Inc., 1988), 49.

26. See, for example, D. Boyarin, "Origen as Theorist of Allegory: Alexandrian Contexts," in *The Cambridge Companion to Allegory*, ed. R. Copeland and P. Struck (New York: Cambridge University Press, 2010), 39–54.

27. "Clement follow[ed] Paul in identifying Christ crucified as the one part of Scripture to be taken literally. All else was to be interpreted figuratively as leading to the finality of the incarnate and crucified Lord." E. Osborn, "Early Christian Philosophers: Justin, Irenaeus, Clement of Alexandria, Tertullian," in *History of Western Philosophy of Religion*, ed. G. Oppy and N. Trakakis (Durham: Acumen, 2009), 1.192.

28. G. Keith, "Can Anything Good Come out of Allegory? The Cases of Origen and Augustine," *Evangelical Quarterly* 70 (1998): 39.

29. Mayer, "Clement of Rome and His Use of Scripture," *Concordia Theological Monthly* 42 (1971): 536.

30. For an evangelical treatment of the issue, see G. Allison's chapter on "the interpretation of Scripture" in his *Historical Theology: An Introduction to Christian Doctrine* (Grand Rapids: Zondervan, 2011), 162–86.

precisely because they had an extraordinarily *high* view of the Bible that it occurred to them to resort to allegorical methods in the first place. What was this "high" view exactly? In a nutshell, the early churches believed that every time they engaged any passage in Scripture, they had a spiritual obligation to find a *christological* meaning buried somewhere within a text. If no christological meaning could be found on a text's "surface," then it behooved the exegete to look beneath the surface.

Early Christian exegetes had every assurance that the meaning of all Scripture, whether hidden or not, *is* Christ.[31] What I propose is that scriptural authority needs to be re-cast today in light of how exegetes deliberately set out to make Christ known through Scripture. Or put another way, I do not think it wrong to say that Scripture's believing readers *confer authority upon the Bible* by their constant act of directing and re-directing Scripture toward the possibility of being read "christocentrically."

4. Linking with the Ontological Authority of Christ Is the Hermeneutical Outcome of Allegory/Typology

In order to be successful, then, biblical exegetes required something *like* an allegorical procedure. To accomplish christological readings, allegorical methods had to be used. In many ways, only allegory had a chance at doing hermeneutical justice to a corpus of writings with such unique status as the Bible. In antiquity, allegory was especially applied to those texts that were believed to carry messages too profound to be communicated literally. Hence, for many Greek thinkers, the use of allegorical method was mainly restricted to works of poetry. For example, when the third-century philosopher, Porphyry, challenged Origen's use of allegory on the OT, one of his main complaints was that "they [Christian exegetes] boast that the things that are said clearly by Moses are enigmas, and they ascribe inspiration to those sayings as if they were oracles full of hidden mysteries."[32]

Some modern researchers have emphasized that there appears to have been a difference between what Greek thinkers expected of their texts and what Christians anticipated of theirs. Whitman, for example, offers the

---

31. One example of this is found in a patristic interpretation of Revelation 5 that explains that one of the reasons Christ is the only one worthy to open the two-sided scroll is because, without Christ, none of the Scriptures will make sense.

32. Cited in J. Cook, "Porphyry's Attempted Demolition of Christian Allegory," *International Journal of the Platonic Tradition* 2 (2008): 3.

following contrast between a Greek allegorical outlook and a Hellenistic-Jewish one:

> For Greek exegetes, the poetry of Homer and Hesiod is a diverting fiction. However inspired, it remains subject to the more rigorous discipline of philosophy, which transforms mere stories into facts. By contrast when a different text, the Bible, is allegorized by Hellenized Jews, a reversal of priorities takes place. Because the Word of God, unlike the fictions of the Greek poets, is itself sacred and perfect, its interpretation can be only a form of inferior knowledge, not full knowledge. Accordingly, to apply philosophic interpretation to the Bible means not to place the text at the service of philosophy, but to place philosophy at the service of the text. This change offers at least the promise of a new logic and integrity to the "literal" level, a need that was reaching a critical stage in the Greek tradition with the Stoics.[33]

Inerrantist evangelicals, however, have become less interested in ancient Hellenistic-Jewish (and especially Christian) *anagogy* as they are in ancient biblical *history*.[34] Evangelical biblical scholars in particular insist that Christian allegory (or as some prefer, "typology"[35]) would not have negated the *historicity* of the literal sense. Even if we were to insist on a position like this, we would still have to keep in mind that: "History, in the sense of historicity and factuality, is a predominantly modern concern, generated by the Reformation and the Enlightenment. The ancients had their own interest in history, but it was not ours, and they made no self-conscious connection between history and typology of the kind proposed."[36]

---

33. J. Whitman, *Allegory: The Dynamics of an Ancient and Medieval Technique* (Cambridge, MA: Harvard University Press, 1987), 61.

34. Consider, for example, how an entire team of inerrantists got together to argue against Kent Sparks' proposals set forth in *God's Word in Human Words: An Evangelical Appropriation of Critical Biblical Scholarship* (Grand Rapids: Baker, 2008) and emphasize the importance of history. See J. Hoffmeier and D. Magary, ed., *Do Historical Matters Matter to Faith?: A Critical Appraisal of Modern and Postmodern Approaches to Scripture* (Wheaton, IL: Crossway, 2012).

35. Again, the two terms can be fruitfully seen as more or less synonymous. Compare M. Simonetti, "Allegory-Typology," in *Encyclopedia of Ancient Christianity*, ed. T. Oden and J. Elowsky (Downers Grove, IL: InterVarsity, 2014), 1.86–87.

36. F. Young, "Typology," in *Crossing the Boundaries: Essays in Biblical Interpretation in Honour of Michael D. Goulder*, ed. S. Porter, P. Joyce, and D. Orton (New York: Brill, 1994), 34. She explains further: "The attempt to define typology through associating it closely with historicity and event must be deemed to have failed. I have become more and more convinced that modern perception of what the ancients were doing in their

As with all texts upon which the allegorical methods were practiced, the Old Testament was received by believing communities as being "deficient in meaning and therefore in need of a supplement."[37] Scripture's interpretive supplement, it should be noted, can stem from any inter-textual knowledge that seemed helpful for elucidating a particular biblical text. In other words, the exegete's inter-textual store of knowledge was deliberately applied to scriptural readings with hopes of discovering deeper meanings for the selected passage.[38] As H. Boersma observes, "Figural or anagogical interpretation was, for the Fathers, the way to do justice to the spiritual reality that one encountered by reading on the mountain, in the presence of Christ."[39]

The inerrantist view of Scripture that many evangelicals espouse today could hardly be more different from the "inerrantist" views evinced in writings of theologians who were living in earlier times.[40] For one thing, Christian allegorists, such as Clement, Origen, and Augustine, "faced the dilemma of trying to justify interpretive authority in the context of ongoing interpretive supplements that can have no final closure, the seemingly endless rewriting of texts in a chain of commentary that can never be arrested. The interpreter can never capture, once and for all, the univocal *logos* stripped of its textual representations."[41] In almost every way, the Church Fathers were operating from within a markedly different literary culture than our own. In the early church, "Scripture was meant not primarily to teach us something about the past, but to draw us into the mystery of Christ."[42]

If this is even partially right, then it becomes apparent that some contemporary inerrantist authors are conflating the Bible's "truthfulness" with its "authority" because they think that part of the ground for establishing the Bible's authority is, among other things, its infallible ability to describe how things really are.[43] One example of this is found in Davis' observa-

---

exegesis has been seriously distorted by what might be called 'the Daniélou definition of typology.'"

37. M. Irvine, *The Making of Textual Culture: 'Grammatica' and Literary Theory 350–1100* (New York: Cambridge University Press, 1994), 245.

38. Irvine calls this the "culture encyclopedia." Irvine, *Making*, 245.

39. H. Boersma, "Up the Mountain with the Fathers: Evangelical *Ressourcement* of Early Christian Doctrine," *Canadian Theological Review* (2012): 10.

40. See Bovell, *Rehabilitating Inerrancy*, 118–21.

41. Irvine, *Making*, 247.

42. Boersma, "Up the Mountain," 10.

43. Compare Thiselton's observations regarding Hodge's reaction to Bushnell's appeal to metaphor: "Hodge reacted by claiming the whole of the bible was 'propositional'

tions regarding a person's "psychological attitude" toward statements they take to be true. According to Davis, "we commit ourselves to believe [true statements] (together with all propositions entailed by them), we accept their propositional content, we 'trust' them, we 'lay ourselves open' to them. That is, we allow our noetic structures and behavior to be influenced by them." After stating this, Davis proceeds to draw an analogy that seeks to apply observations regarding true statements generally to the "truth" contained in Christian Scriptures:

> [W]hen we say, "The Bible is true," [w]e mean that our attitude towards the Bible is such that we believe what it says, we trust it, we lay ourselves open to it. We allow our noetic structures and beliefs to be influenced by it. Such an attitude will include, but not by any means be limited to, accepting the truth (in the paradigmatic [i.e. realist] sense) of the assertions that we find in it. . . . If we take the Bible to be true, we trust it to guide our lives. . . . In short, we *submit* to the Bible. We place ourselves under its theological authority.[44]

Contrast Davis' straightforward *propositional* approach with Thiselton's more subtle *hermeneutical* approach, which helps show how an approach like Davis' predisposes believers to "submitting" to the Bible in inappropriate ways: "Arguably then biblical authority remains an *ontological given*, because its basis resides in the sovereignty and grace of God, but also its derivative *currency* resides in its appropriation as an effective communicative event or act whereby believing readers live out their response to this authority."[45] Or to put it another way, what believers are *submitting* to is the ontological lordship of Christ and not the propositional lordship of the Bible, and it is the *former* kind of submission that leads us to "genuine wrestling, search and struggle, in expectancy of a divine event of 'speaking' to a ready heart" as we read the Bible and hear the Bible being read.[46]

---

and 'cognitive.'" A. Thiselton, *Thiselton on Hermeneutics: Collected Works with New Essays* (Grand Rapids: Eerdmans, 2006), 631.

44. S. Davis, "The Bible Is True," in *A Reader in Contemporary Philosophical Theology*, ed. O. Crisp (New York: T & T Clark, 2009), 28.

45. Thiselton, *Thiselton on Hermeneutics*, 632.

46. Thiselton, *Thiselton on Hermeneutics*, 633.

5. "Post-Resurrection": Establishing a Hermeneutic Context for Christ Appearing to People

What I am trying to do is rethink how the authority of the Christian Bible (Old and New Testaments taken together) is both extrinsically and intrinsically tied to Christ's resurrection. Along the way, I will pause to consider what the resurrection *is* and how Christ's resurrection in particular may impinge upon the authority of our scriptural documents. In what follows, I speculate on how the post-resurrection mindset was first introduced to some of the biblical writers and suggest that the Bible's authority 1) initially resided in its comprisal of traditional reflections on and applications of mystical experiences had "in" Christ or "in the spirit" by various groups and individuals in the early churches after Christ was resurrected, and 2) is constantly conferred upon Scripture by its believing recipients in *their* sustained, hermeneutical interactions with it, which collectively comprise faithful, anagogical attempts to both initially direct and continually redirect the Scriptures *toward* Christ.[47]

I do not see any other way to proceed that would not involve some degree of speculation, but there is no question in my mind that an exercise like this will still yield real, spiritual results. What I am going to try to do specifically is ground the authority of the Scriptures in actual mystical experiences of groups and individuals in the early churches. The experiences early believers had, I posit, involved altered states of consciousness, and were likely had by only a handful of biblical writers. Still, whatever the actual number of believers were involved, it was sufficient to establish the "core message" of Christian Scripture. The New Testament, collected over time, was—at first—an informal attempt to bring together for the benefit of the network of churches what was thought to be known about Jesus Christ. The protracted process of canonization can be seen as a concerted effort to faithfully gather in one collection the accumulated wisdom of the ancient churches that spelled out the significance of Jesus' appearing to his disciples after he had been crucified (resurrection) and what impact these appearances should have on the new communities then forming, the majority of which had never seen Jesus, whether while alive or after being crucified.

For my portrayal of *inspiration* (see chapter one above) the post-resurrection perspective is crucial. The same also holds for my account of

---

47. I will have more to say as well during my discussion of the Bible's "internal" authority in the next chapter.

The Authority of Scripture

Scripture's contemporary *authority*. Before the resurrection, the Old Testament's authority, whatever it might have been, had to have been different in kind from the authority it began to possess as post-resurrection frameworks became available. For Christians, there really is a "problem of the Old Testament"—at least for any Christian who thinks the Old Testament demands to be understood in pre-resurrection terms because "[i]n time a new book, the Christian New Testament, [came to stand] between the interpreter and the Jewish Bible."[48]

The NT canon began to take shape at precisely a time when "trends toward summarization, regularization and codification" of knowledge in the wider Roman Empire were taking place. D. Groh observes: "Around A.D. 200 the Severan Jurists are at work on the Roman law. Around the same time an important codification of the Mishna is made. At exactly this point in time, Peter Brown claims the cumulative wisdom of Greek culture was brought together and systematized in handbooks and encyclopedias which were to be used throughout the Middle Ages."[49] By way of comparison, Greenwald says of Marcion's efforts to establish a NT canon, that "had he been pagan, he could have been included devoid of distinguishing characteristics in our list of second century epitomators and collectors."[50]

Greenwald and others see important parallels in the contemporaneous formation of the NT and the Mishnah. Stroumsa, for example, identifies fundamental connections between both compilations:

> Both texts, then, the New Testament and the Mishnah, can be considered as two kinds of 'meta-Tanakh,' as it were, two parallel works coming after the Tanakh, deeply different in content but rather similar in function. It is remarkable that both texts became crystallized and canonized more or less at the same period, toward the end of the second century, or at the latest in the early third century.[51]

Simply put, the NT is a collection of the best witnesses the churches had available at a time in cultural history when each discipline was consolidating

---

48. R. Wilken, "Review of *Early Biblical Interpretation* by J. Kugel and R. Greer," *Theological Studies* 48 (1987): 538.

49. See D. Groh, "Hans von Campenhausen on Canon: Positions and Problems," *Interpretation* 28 (1974): 343.

50. M. Greenwald, "The New Testament Canon and the Mishnah: Consolidation of Knowledge in the Second Century C. E." (Ph.D. diss., Boston University, 1989), 154.

51. G. Stroumsa, *Hidden Wisdom: Esoteric Traditions and the Roots of Christian Mysticism*, 2nd ed. (Leiden: Brill, 2005), 90.

the knowledge it had accumulated up to that point. As Löfstedt helpfully reminds us, "There is no need to mystify the creation of the NT canon."[52] If there *is* something to mystify, it is how Christ was able to appear to his early followers after being crucified. As for the NT documents, however, these can be received as attempts to establish a post-resurrection framework for understanding the significance of the experiences. They outline the hermeneutical context from within which believers can conceive of God, namely, how much love he has for us given that Christ, God's Son, has been revealed.

6. John the Revelator, a Post-Resurrection Exemplar?

Regarding Christ's appearing to people as being the catalyst for New Testament Christianity, the closest thing that comes to mind that we might try to compare it to is the "heavenly journeys" described in some of the apocalyptic literature of second temple Judaism. What I propose—and this is the kind of speculation that will need to be done if we are going to make any progress—is that we imagine that the way Jesus appeared to Paul and other apostles was not so different from the way in which he appeared to the prophet at Patmos, John, the writer of Revelation. If this assumption is not too much to presume, then the book of Revelation, a book subjected to the worst kind of end-times speculation, actually provides a glimpse of *how* Jesus communicated with the earliest believers after his crucifixion. What we have in Revelation, I submit, is a phenomenological description (expressed apocalyptically) of the resurrected Jesus interacting with the earliest believers. This first-person account may be fruitfully combined with the other, third-person accounts that have been passed down by the anonymous hagiographers who were behind the gospels and the Acts, among others.

In Revelation chapter 1, John explains that he was "in the spirit" on the Lord's Day. It seems safe to say that this phrase draws attention to an important, ecstatic component—suggesting he was perhaps *in the habit of* "being in the spirit"—that characterized first century Christianity, a component, we might add, that inerrantist Evangelicalism seems only too

---

52. Löfstedt, "Defence," 65. It is not necessary, for example, to follow K. Vanhoozer's canonical linguistic theology and "[insist] that the canon is the result of a divine covenantal initiative." Vanhoozer, *The Drama of Doctrine: A Canonical-linguistic Approach to Christian Theology* (Louisville, KY: Westminster John Knox, 2005), 146.

willing to overlook.[53] The prophet John at Patmos writes that he heard a voice like a trumpet. Some who have had similar visions might suggest that the voice he heard was the voice of the vision itself, somehow announcing its own arrival to the person experiencing it. The vision sometimes delivers a message that prepares the visionary for what is about to follow; it sets up the vision's content, so to speak.[54] In this case, the announcement instructs John to write down what he sees and to send what he writes to the churches. The content presented in this vision happens to be nothing other than the revelation of Jesus Christ himself.

The revelations of Jesus Christ that were received during the apostles' (and others') mystical experiences appear to have been given to them exclusively and "not to the world," as it were. This means, I suggest, that the divine communication involved in these altered states of consciousness allowed the intended recipients—*and them alone*—to be "tuned in" to the appearing of the resurrected Jesus. So when the author of the book of Acts, for example, states, "After his suffering he presented himself alive to them by many convincing proofs" we might suppose that others who may have been standing by could have been completely unaware that the resurrected Christ was standing in their midst.[55]

For example, there is an oft-discussed discrepancy among the three accounts given in the book of Acts that describe what Paul's companions

---

53. Compare E. Sharpe, "'I Was in the Spirit on the Lord's Day': Reflections on Ecstatic Religion in the New Testament," in *The Concept of the Spirit*, Prudentia Supplement, ed. D. W. Dockrill and R. G. Tanner (Sydney: University of Sydney, 1985), 119-31. Although caustic, I understand how Watts could remark: "A Christianity which is not basically mystical must become either a political ideology or a mindless Fundamentalism. . . . for lack of the mystical element, both trends fall back on the Bible as their basic inspiration—and it has always struck me that biblical idolatry is one of the most depressing and sterile fixations of the religious mind." A. Watts, *Behold the Spirit: A Study in the Necessity of Mystical Religion* (New York: Vintage, 1971), xiii.

54. In Gen 1, for example, the "let there be light," etc. was not said by anyone but rather somehow integrally part of what was transpiring, an aspect of the event itself transpiring. Compare R. Guardini, *The Lord*, (Washington, D. C.: Regnery, 1954), 563: ". . . that was the voice of the vision itself."

55. Again, compare Guardini, *The Lord*, 570, where he describes John of Patmos: "What he saw was nothing visible to the natural eyes of anyone living among natural objects . . ." Paul's claim that Jesus appeared to a multitude of 500 presumably occurred during worship and/or prayer. The experience of seeing the resurrected Christ is evidence of his being alive in some "alternate" reality. Compare J. Pilch, "Appearances of the Risen Jesus in Cultural Context: Experiences of Alternate Reality," *Biblical Theology Bulletin* 28 (1998): 52-60.

saw and/or heard when Jesus appeared to him on the way to Damascus. Stanley seems anxious to reassure readers that Paul's companions were "sure that someone was present," but his apology is unnecessary. The main point of recounting Paul's experience three times is "to insist that Paul did see Christ" and that "[h]is experience was, then, specifically the same as that of the Apostles on the various occasions of Christ's post-Resurrection appearances."[56] In what follows, I refer to the visionaries to whom Christ appeared as "mystics."

7. Jesus Appearing to People and New Testament Mysticism

In their attempts to integrate their experiences of Christ appearing to them and their everyday ministries, the early Christian "mystics" plumbed their mystical experiences of the post-resurrection Jesus for practical implications. From these, they were able to find new cultural perspectives by which the newly founded Christian communities could come to understand themselves, especially in the face of their surrounding, non-Christian cultures. In other words, what the post-resurrection appearances provided was—in addition to any specific commands given to them by the Lord (1 Cor 7.10; 14.35, 37)—an appropriate perspective from which to approach a host of issues occupying Christian believers at the time.

Hurtado has argued that the "powerful religious experiences [of the earliest Christians were] perceived by the recipients as 'revelations'" and that these are "important chief historical factors that helped the religious innovations of the movement."[57] Although I would hesitate to speak of "innovations," I would certainly remain content to observe that the post-resurrection appearances were what compelled the earliest Christians to continue speaking of Jesus as if he were alive and to draw the conclusion, in fact, that he had been resurrected from the dead by God. What the earliest Christians came to understand was that Christ's message—that the Kingdom of God is at hand—is one that God still wanted the world to hear (compare Jn 14.12).

Accordingly, the evangelist behind the Gospel of Mark, for example, sought "*to influence as large an audience as possible*, including even the most

---

56. D. Stanley, "Paul's Conversion in Acts: Why the Three Accounts?" *Catholic Biblical Quarterly* 15 (1953): 329.

57. L. Hurtado, "Religious Experience and Religious Innovation in the New Testament," *Journal of Religion* 80 (2000): 183.

inexperienced readers." Toward this end, the Markan evangelist produced a story about Jesus' life, death, and resurrection that was both Jewish-prophetic *and* Hellenistic-epic and that had resurrection as its main theme. Fullmer explains further, "Mark's novelistic stylistics are strikingly rudimentary in comparison to most Hellenistic historians—indeed, even in comparison to most popular literature. . . . Through this preference for even the simplest of novelistic forms, the author of the Gospel communicates his concern to persuade as wide an audience as possible—indeed, to proclaim his good news 'to all nations' (Mk 13.10)."[58] Though little understood at the time—the Gospel ends with the women being so afraid that they didn't tell anyone—the urgent message to disseminate was that, in spite of the fact that Jesus had been crucified and died, he was somehow still very much alive.

Well before the time when the evangelists penned the gospels, the burgeoning NT literature was comprised of epistles written (or perhaps more likely, dictated) by mystics for broader audiences with hopes of providing instruction, encouragement, and edification to the recipients. A paradigm was being set for the later NT writers by Paul's own genre-transformation of "the private letter of friendship into a community letter" that proclaimed new life in Christ.[59] If it is true that the first NT canon was essentially a collection of "Pauline" epistles,[60] then it would not be unreasonable to conceive of the pseudonymous letters, the anonymous four Gospels and Acts, and perhaps portions of the book of Revelation as later attempts to *work backwards*, as it were, from 1) traditions/remembrances that originated with people mystically experiencing the risen Christ; 2) a body of dominical teachings and sayings passed along by faithful disciples; and 3) a Pauline corpus, that sought to foster in converts the virtues that come with the Christian ethos as far as he understood it and insofar as Christ had taught it to him.

Meade draws attention to the "testamentary approach" that later NT writings introduce to post-apostolic thinking about Scripture (in 2 Peter, the Pastorals, Revelation, the Gospel of John, for example). The testamentary genre seen in the "Pauline" epistles, the book of Revelation (which, interestingly enough, presents seven testamentary epistles together in one

---

58. P. Fullmer, *Resurrection in Mark's Literary-Historical Perspective* (New York: T & T Clark 2007), 206, 207.

59. Thiessen, *The New Testament: A Literary History* (Minneapolis: Fortress, 2012), 61.

60. See S. Porter, "When and How Was the Pauline Canon Compiled? An Assessment of Theories," in *The Pauline Canon*, ed. S. Porter (Boston: Brill, 2004), 95–127.

book), and the fourth evangelist's account of the life and teachings of Jesus are provided anonymously and even pseudonymously as part of post-apostolic efforts to stabilize the apostles' teachings after they had passed away.[61]

The earliest strands of the NT had their beginnings in the efforts of mystic authors to both communicate and apply what knowledge they had gained from revelatory experiences of the risen Christ. Surely Löfstedt is on to something when he writes, "We don't have to assume that the New Testament could not have been any larger than it is."[62] It could easily have been the case that there were other writings besides that were both apostolic and authoritative that ultimately proved less useful as the circles of believers widened. Alternately, it is conceivable, then, that there are canonical NT books that, although initially included for good and legitimate reasons, will not prove ultimately useful to later posterity. Such books must be creatively re-interpreted if they are to remain spiritually profitable in light of redemptive-historical (i.e., eschatological) developments along with other developments in culture.

8. Traditions Trying to Make Sense of Jesus Appearing to People

The NT makes clear that the post-resurrection appearances of Christ were absolutely central to the origins of Christianity. Perhaps these appearances can also be made to feature more prominently in our understandings of the NT's external authority. In 1 Cor 15.3–5, for example, we have a very early formulaic expression of the Christian faith that, although often plumbed for its emphasis on *resurrection*, seems actually to be working backwards from an even deeper emphasis on *Christ's appearing to people after being dead*:[63]

---

61. See D. Meade, "Ancient Near Eastern Apocalypticism and the Origins of the New Testament Canon of Scripture," in *The Bible as Human Witness to Divine Revelation: Hearing the Word of God through Historically Dissimilar Traditions*, ed. R. Heskett and B. Irwin (New York: T & T Clark International, 2010), 302–21.

62. See Löfstedt, "Defence," 65–66.

63. H. J. de Jonge surmises that this traditional material was in circulation by the year 50 CE and that reports of Jesus appearing to Peter date back to the year 35 CE. See de Jonge, "Visionary Experience and the Historical Origins of Christianity," in *Resurrection in the New Testament: Festschrift J. Lambrecht*, ed. R. Bieringer, et. al. (Leuven: Leuven University Press, 2002), 40–41.

Christ died for our sins, in accordance with the Scriptures;

he was buried

he was raised on the third day, in accordance with the Scriptures;

he appeared to Cephas and then to the twelve.[64]

The formula tersely presents two basic ideas: 1) To *understand* Christ's death and his resurrection, Christians should formulate our explanations "in accordance with the Scriptures;" 2) To *prove* that Christ died and that he was resurrected, we are to look respectively to the fact that he was buried and to the fact that he appeared to his disciples.[65] This is not only the historical kernel that religious historians must start out with to reconstruct the origins of Christianity,[66] it is also the religio-cultural kernel that believing Christians should eventually go back to if they want to better imagine how their faith was culturally conceived: 1) Christ died; and 2) Christ appeared to his apostles after having died.[67]

The Acts of the Apostles is suggestive of a similar stance with respect to the resurrection and its "proof": "After his suffering he presented himself alive to them by many convincing proofs, appearing to them over the course of forty days and speaking about the kingdom of God" (Acts 1.3). The appearances are what prompted the movement to continue Jesus' ministry, the mystery of "resurrection" being invoked to explain it. To help illustrate this, K. Bailey draws an illuminating parallel between John the Baptist and Jesus. In both cases, Bailey notes, "A proclaimer of the gospel made powerful enemies because of his proclamation. That proclaimer was unjustly imprisoned. . . . An innocent man was brutally murdered (justice

---

64. For this translation, see E. Schweizer, *Jesus* (trans. D. Green; Atlanta: John Knox, 1971), 94.

65. Schweizer, *Jesus*, 94. Compare K. Bailey, *Paul through Mediterranean Eyes: Cultural Studies in 1 Corinthians* (Downers Grove, IL: InterVarsity, 2011), 428–31.

66. Compare M. Smith, "Ascent to the Heavens and the Beginning of Christianity," *Eranos-Jahrbuch* 50 (1981): 404: who claims that the "main facts" are "[Jesus] was a Jewish miracle man active in Palestine during the late twenties and/or the early thirties, who attracted so great a following that the authorities feared he might become the center of a revolutionary movement. They therefore had him crucified and his followers began to see him risen from the dead." The "minimal facts approach" to apologetics tries to use history to support a Christian understanding of resurrection. This approach was made popular by G. Habermas and was subsequently taken up by his student, M. Licona. For a popular treatment, see G. Habermas and M. Licona, *The Case for the Resurrection of Jesus* (Grand Rapids: Kregel, 2004).

67. Compare Pilch, "Appearances of Jesus," 58–59.

was violated). . . . Disciples of the victim took the body and buried it." The critical *dis*similarity, however, is that in John's case: "Resurrection was supposed by Herod, but nothing came of it;" in Jesus' case, *Jesus appeared to his followers* "and that made all the difference."[68]

9. "According to the Scriptures": Looking to the OT to Make Sense of Jesus Appearing to People

With such an emphasis on Jesus appearing to people after dying by crucifixion, mystically described—both in the NT *and in the traditions behind the NT*—in terms of "resurrection," questions immediately arose as to how OT Scriptures could continue to be used by early Christians. Although I cannot satisfactorily address this topic here, it seems appropriate to offer a few tentative remarks.

OT Scriptures were authoritative for the earliest Christians because Jesus, being Jewish, accepted OT Scriptures as authoritative.[69] It is in the context of and continuity with the religious world of OT Scriptures—and especially its various interpretive traditions—that Jesus understood his message and carried out his healing and miracle-working ministry. Oegema explains that in addition to believing in resurrection and accepting the belief that God was both creator and judge of his creation, Jesus "advocated belief in the love of God for all of humankind, in the Torah as the expression of God's will, in God's call to become holy as God is, and in the notion that the final consequence of love may be suffering for one's neighbor,

---

68. Bailey, *Paul*, 429-30. Perkins draws attention to the fact that Jesus' disciples did not come to bury the body, suggesting that Jesus being crucified says more about his social class than about the "gravity of the crime." See P. Perkins, "The Resurrection of Jesus of Nazareth," in *Studying the Historical Jesus: Evaluations of the State of Current Research*, ed. B. Chilton and C. Evans (New York: Brill, 1994), 431-32.

69. This is not the place to get caught up in issues surrounding the closing of a canon for the OT. Conservatives are still concerned to argue that Scripture (the MT?) has, practically speaking at least, *always* been around for Christianity to work with. The same goes for the NT. C. Blaising insists, for example, that "the church was carrying forward by tradition what had always been the case." See Blaising, "William J. Abraham's *Canon and Criterion in Christian Theology: From the Fathers to Feminism*," *Churchman* 115 (2001): 105. Compare M. Kruger's move to dissolve the "scripture/canon" distinction, to make sure that the NT can already be a factor at the earliest stages of Christianity. See M. Kruger, *The Question of Canon: Challenging the Status Quo in the New Testament Debate* (Downers Grove: InterVarsity, 2013).

as God also suffers for humankind. Jesus's theology was therefore mainly based on theology that can also be found in the Hebrew Bible."[70]

Secondly, OT Scriptures were authoritative for the earliest Christians on account of the earliest Christians' own cultural upbringing in the context of ancient Jewish spirituality. Jesus' disciples did not really need Jesus to approve of the OT Scriptures. Perhaps, one could even venture to say that they would have considered it suspect had he *not* approved of the OT Scriptures. Moreover, to the extent that they found it possible to maintain some continuity with the OT Scriptures—which included, by extension, various of its interpretive traditions—they remained committed to the prospect of coming to terms with Jesus appearing to them (after his crucifixion) in light of them.

A new appreciation of who Jesus is in light of his appearances to people after being crucified was eventually incorporated into narrative traditions surrounding Jesus himself. These traditions began to circulate along with short summaries of his teachings, stories about his ministry, and stories about his disciples. But even more importantly, the early Christians, including the NT writers, came to see Jesus as the focal point for God's dealings with humanity. To help them articulate what momentous, eschatological developments they thought had taken place in Jesus' life, death, resurrection, and ascension, "Christians began thus to use [the OT Scriptures] 'historically' (as we should say) [because] they had actually found in Jesus of Nazareth the climax of the long story of God's dealings with his people."[71] Moule observes that the early church understood that "the pure stream of God's purposes" were "perfectly achieved" in Jesus: "it was inevitable, therefore, that the great biblical passages about the ideal people of God, as well as those about their ideal representatives, should begin to be drawn together round Jesus, as a magnet collects iron fillings."[72]

Evangelicals, perhaps motivated by their doctrinal adherence to inerrancy, often seek to objectively "find" Jesus in the OT with hopes of establishing maximal prophetic continuity between the OT and the NT. Bateman, Bock, and Johnston, for example, set out to "[*discover*] who Jesus the Messiah is, and how Jesus himself, in the progress of revelation, fits

---

70. G. Oegema, *Apocalyptic Interpretation of the Bible: Apocalypticism and Biblical Interpretation in Early Judaism, the Apostle Paul, the Historical Jesus, and Their Reception History* (New York: T & T Clark, 2012), 93–94.

71. C. F. D. Moule, *The Birth of the New Testament* (New York: Harper and Row, 1962), 68.

72. Moule, *Birth*, 68–69.

together the pieces of God's messianic puzzle."[73] In his monograph on the same subject, M. Rydelnik explains that there *must* be a close link between Jesus' ministry and the OT's messianic prophecies: "The relationship between Old Testament prophecy and messianic fulfillment is essential to a theological defense of the messiahship of Jesus of Nazareth."[74]

Although this is certainly one way to interpret Christ's ministry "in accordance to the Scriptures," I suggest that heavy-handed, bibliologically-motivated approaches to finding Jesus in the OT impose upon Scripture a "predictive" capacity that it cannot historically bear.[75] A saner approach might be to content ourselves with the observation that Jesus' disciples only "found" Jesus in Scripture *after* he appeared to them post-Easter. In other words, "[w]hen the community was forced to find words to express the significance of Jesus for the world, it was naturally compelled to use terms and images that were meaningful and comprehensible in their contemporary environment."[76] The disciples began to understand their Scriptures backwards, as it were, with the events that befell Jesus always in the forefront of their minds. On the basis of what had happened to Jesus and how he continued appearing to people after dying, it seemed almost as if "Jesus was every Jewish hero rolled into one."[77]

For our part, rather than insisting ad hoc on what *predictive* qualities the OT has, there would be far less contrivances involved if we chose instead to adopt a more pragmatic view, a view that openly acknowledges the creative and imaginative uses to which the NT tradents put their Scriptures within their cultural context. As Harrington demonstrates, "[i]n first-century Judaism there was no uniform eschatological scenario and no single doctrine of the Messiah."[78] Several interpretative traditions were

---

73. H. Bateman, D. Bock, and G. Johnston, *Jesus the Messiah: Tracing the Promises, Expectations, and Coming of Israel's King* (Grand Rapids: Kregel, 2012), 30.

74. Rydelnik, *The Messianic Hope: Is the Hebrew Bible Really Messianic?* (Nashville, TN: Broadman and Hollman, 2010), 32.

75. One could be forgiven for suspecting an anxiety in Rydelnik's theological plea since he himself discloses that "messianic prophecy was the means God used to bring me to faith in Jesus the Messiah." See Rydelnik, *Messianic Hope*, 11. This raises the interesting question of whether what God uses to bring someone to faith must be a part of what *keeps* a person in faith?

76. Schweizer, *Jesus*, 83.

77. Adapted from K. Sparks claim that *Matthew's* Jesus is "every Jewish hero rolled into one." See Sparks, "Gospel as Conquest: Mosaic Typology in Matthew 28: 16-20," *Catholic Biblical Quarterly* 68 (2006): 662.

78. D. Harrington, "Afterlife Expectations in Pseudo-Philo, 4 Ezra, and 2 Baruch,

in circulation at the time, each poised to be developed further and taken in whatever direction the hour required. Not only this, but the very texts themselves upon which the interpretive traditions were based became "'fluid' and variant under the influence of such interpretive dynamics," variant readings being given preference according to the demands of various groups of exegetes.[79]

10. The NT as Trying to Make Sense of Jesus Appearing to People

From this kind of perspective, the NT message can be received as the collective effort of early Christian communities to express what the churches had learnt from the post-Easter appearances of the disciples. This would presumably include whatever Jesus was thought to have said to them when he appeared to them. The experiences of these teachings would be expressed through "the latent discourse of a culture."[80] As Schweizer observes, "The only Bible the community has is the Old Testament. This is where it must look for information when bothered by questions."[81] Accordingly, the followers of Jesus drew on the OT materials not only to make sense of Jesus' appearing to them but also to answer their questions with respect to how they should now understand what was happening from their in-the-process-of-being-developed post-resurrection perspective on who Jesus was, where "[t]he hard reality of history is mediated by the imaginative projection of communal or individual self-understanding."[82]

From the perspective of a believer, then, it seems right to follow Schweizer's observation and look to the OT for help with understanding the significance of Jesus' life, death, resurrection, and ascension, but Rydelnik and others would arguably be wrong in supposing that the OT is where *outsiders* could look for answers about Jesus should *they* ever be "bothered

---

and Their Implications for the New Testament," in *Resurrection in the New Testament*, 29.

79. J. Tabor, "Are You the One? The Textual Dynamics of Messianic Self-Identity," in *Knowing the End from the Beginning: The Prophetic, the Apocalyptic, and their Relationships*, ed. L. Grabbe and R. Haak (New York: T & T Clark International, 2003), 180.

80. See Pilch, "Appearances of Jesus," 54.

81. See Schweizer, *Jesus*, 55.

82. J. Tabor, "Are you the One?," 188. Tabor points to the conviction of the charismatic leader as "furnish[ing] the apologetic power." For our discussion, it would be Jesus' appearances that motivated the early churches' christological readings of the OT.

by questions." After all, not even the disciples were able to "see" Jesus in the OT![83] As Cranfield observes: "The early church, convinced that Jesus had been raised, certainly searched the Old Testament for passages which could be taken to foretell the Resurrection: but there is no reason to believe that the Old Testament had suggested to the disciples, before the Easter Day, any hope of this sort."[84] Not until Jesus appeared to them post-Easter and the Holy Spirit indwelt them (again post-Easter) did Jesus' disciples begin to pursue how to apply scriptural passages *to him*.[85]

After Christ's death and resurrection, Christians began explicitly reading the OT to answer a set of questions that had never been put to it before: "Who is Jesus?" "What should we make of the fact that he was crucified?" "How can one make sense of the fact that, in spite of his being crucified, he appeared to his followers after being buried?" The new, Christian, "messianic" readings that the disciples were in the process of developing began by putting *the specific question of Jesus* to the OT, thereby introducing a radically new hermeneutical impetus to their Second Temple exegetical approaches to Scripture.

In other words, the earliest churches began deliberately fashioning OT interpretations that were sufficiently christological for establishing a new hermeneutical space, one in which "the new reality of Christ" could more easily fit. Over time, this became the standard practice. As Wilken notes, "Following St. Paul, the Church Fathers argued that a surface reading of the Old Testament, what Origen calls the 'plain' meaning, missed what was most important in the Bible: Jesus Christ."[86] Of course, it did not take long for questions to arise as to whether this Christian method of reading Jesus back into the Septuagint could count as a legitimate interpretation of *Jewish* Scripture. Some Christians decided it was not and elected either to forego the OT altogether or, alternately, accept only those OT Scriptures that were

---

83. Compare Mark 9.10, 32, etc.

84. C. E. B. Cranfield, "The Resurrection of Jesus Christ," *Expository Times* 101 (1990): 170.

85. I once heard a Jewish scholar remark on Philip's encounter with the Ethiopian eunuch in Acts 8, insisting that there was no way that the eunuch would have come up with that reading of Isaiah on his own: he must have received that interpretation from Christians. Compare C. Evans and P. Flint, "Introduction," in *Eschatology, Messianism, and the Dead Sea Scrolls*, ed. C. Evans and P. Flint (Grand Rapids: Eerdmans, 1997), 9: "The suffering Messiah is almost certainly absent from the Dead Sea Scrolls, although from time to time some scholars have tried to find it."

86. R. Wilken, "How to Read the Bible," *First Things*, March 2008, <http://www.firstthings.com/article/2008/02/002-how-to-read-the-bible-9>.

amenable to christological interpretation (e.g., Marcion and Ignatius of Antioch, respectively[87]).

Another alternative is that embodied by Jewish groups who dismissed these christological interpretations. Stroumsa explains: "The canonization of the New Testament must thus be seen in direct connection with the fight for the correct interpretation of the Scripture. Now the fight was fiercest between the Christians and the Jews, who argued about the same corpus, the Old Testament. Their argument was essentially of a hermeneutical nature."[88] To be clear, what was at stake was not a mere matter of hermeneutical *method*, but rather a hermeneutical *behavior* (as Stroumsa calls it) that vested the person of Jesus and the events surrounding him with such eschatological significance that the OT Scriptures were now said to receive *their* significance *from Jesus* and not Jesus from the OT—a view of Scripture so different from what preceded it that Stroumsa declares it *revolutionary*.[89]

11. Legitimatizing the OT (plural) by bringing Christ to it

Whether for political or theological purposes (or both),[90] posterity's understanding of Jesus' life, death, resurrection, and ascension, which would include the reception of the apostles' subsequent ministries, became inextricably connected to the OT materials (and, by extension, to their various interpretive traditions). Therefore, the Christian link between the Old and

---

87. Sausane reads Ignatius differently: "When Ignatius says here that to him the Scriptures 'are' Jesus Christ, his passion and resurrection, this should probably not be taken to mean that the passion and resurrection of Christ replace the Old Testament as a new 'Scripture,' but rather that, for Ignatius, the passion and resurrection are the central contents of the Old Testament." Sausane, "Scripture Interpretation in the Second and Third Centuries," in *Hebrew Bible/Old Testament: The History of Its Interpretation, 1.1: Antiquity* (Göttingen: Vandenhoeck & Ruprecht, 1996), 379.

88. Stroumsa, *Hidden Wisdom*, 89.

89. He calls it a "revolution." See G. Stroumsa, "The Christian Hermeneutical Revolution and Its Double Helix," in *The Use of Sacred Books in the Ancient World*, ed. L. V. Rutgers, P. W. van der Horst, et. al. (Leuven: Peeters, 1998), 9–28. Compare Müller: "At first the task had been to legitimatize the Christ faith by reference to Scripture. But in this new situation instead it became necessary *to legitimatize Scripture* by reference to the Christ faith in order to establish its specific Christian significance." M. Müller, "The Reception of the Old Testament in Matthew and Luke-Acts: From Interpretation to Proof from Scripture," *NovT* 43 (2001): 315, italics added.

90. There must have been cultural pressure for Christians to demonstrate their antiquity. Linking to the OT would have been an expedient way to argue for it.

New Testaments is most helpfully conceived as being both too fundamental to allow for the excising of the former from the latter and too loose to prevent a plurality of OT canons from attaching themselves to the NT collection over time. As Rowland explains:

> What the New Testament authors wrote about is the way ancient prophets relate to the present generation and how the key actors in the divine drama, to which they bear witness, are themselves imbued with a sense of vocation and special charisma imitating, and indeed transcending, the prophets of old. *Something special was happening which both linked and set apart the present.*[91]

Accordingly, if the NT is understood as a deposit of the early churches' attempts to understand the significance of Jesus' appearing to people after being crucified, then perhaps believers today should mirror the same attitudes toward the OT material that the NT communities held. One result, I submit, would be that believers today should be flexible in our attitudes regarding the OT material.[92] Just as it seems the formation of the OT canon was a comparatively late development, meaning the boundaries of Scripture were fluid for NT communities, so believers today should be open to the genuine acceptance of a plurality of scriptural canons.[93] According to the outline of biblical authority presented here, different believing communities are free to develop and adopt different OT canons as they see fit

---

91. C. Rowland, "Prophecy and the New Testament," in *Prophecy and the Prophets in Ancient Israel*, ed. J. Day (New York: T & T Clark International, 2010), 411, emphasis added.

92. This includes accepting the prospect (the likelihood?) that the formation of the OT canon was a comparatively late development. See, for example, T. Lim, "A Theory of the Majority Canon," *Expository Times* 124 (2013): 365–73. F. Bovon draws on categories established by ancient writers, suggesting that canonical fluidity followed a more or less identifiable pattern: canonical, apocryphal, and disputed (accepted by some but not by others). See Bovon, "Beyond the Canonical and the Apocryphal Books, the Presence of a Third Category: The Books Useful for the Soul," *Harvard Theological Review* 105 (2012): 125–37.

93. Conservative evangelicals are emphatically against the idea that their canon is not *the* canon in the way they conceive of it theologically. Meade writes that such a position is no longer tenable: "It is time to recognize that the canons of the Roman Catholic and the Eastern churches more accurately reflect the state of first century Christian Scriptures, and that conservative efforts to equate the 'Old Testament' of Jesus and the New Testament apostles with the rabbinic canon of the Hebrew Bible stem from an obsolete Protestant attempt to maintain the doctrine and authentication of Scripture within Scripture, and thus deny the role of the early (Catholic) church." See Meade, "Apocalypticism," 308–9.

for the purposes of understanding Christ as the culmination of God's revelation to humankind. In this context of external authority—the ongoing attempt to explain and come to terms with the fact that Christ appeared to his followers after being crucified—the development and adoption of differing canons by different Christian traditions around the world does not pose a problem. On the contrary, it is just what one would expect. As a consequence, there is no longer a need to speak of the biblical canon *per se*, but rather the biblical canon *accepted by a given community of believers*.

12. Concluding remarks

Any account of biblical authority that theologians offer in the twenty-first century will have to do more to give a satisfactory account of the vast diversity that characterizes both global and historic Christianity. Given my proposal for biblical inspiration outlined in chapter one above, plurality is precisely what Christians should expect, *and they should expect it to go "all the way down."*[94] A contemporary account of biblical authority must face up to the variegated historical and geographical developments that have taken place organically within Christian religion.

Aside from the mystical-theological problem of trying to understand how/why Jesus appeared to followers after being crucified (what early Christians conceived as "resurrection"), an important, *historical* consideration can help us view canonical pluralism in ways that helpfully inform a contemporary construal of biblical authority. From a historical-critical standpoint, distinguishing between a scriptural text and any extra-biblical writing that played a significant role in that text's reception is a historically contingent matter, one that theology still has trouble appreciating.[95] What differentiates the two is precisely the labels we apply and the authority we invest in them. In an earlier piece, I considered how a received interpretation of

---

94. A. Thiselton voices his concern that Christian hermeneuts must always have a "responsible" plurality in view, but he seems somewhat more at ease when he comes to the end of his essay and observes that some of the less fruitful proposals seem to have already run their course. He does see, however, the "dissolution" of hermeneutics as an ever present danger. See Thiselton, "The Future of Biblical Interpretation and Responsible Plurality in Hermeneutics," in *The Future of Biblical Interpretation: Responsible Plurality in Biblical Hermeneutics*, ed. S. Porter and M. Malcolm (Downers Grove, IL: InterVarsity, 2013), 25–26.

95. A notable exception is D. Brown, *Tradition and Imagination: Revelation and Change* (New York: Oxford University Press, 1999).

Scripture (an extra-biblical construct) may be easily distinguished *in theory* from Scripture itself, but is an altogether thornier issue *in practice*.[96] As Dunn has observed, "The authoritative Scripture *is* Scripture interpreted."[97] A practical consequence, then, is that performances of Scripture play a very important part in how the authority of Scripture is conceived.

For Scripture's external authority, then, we might say that the Bible represents the early churches' best efforts to display their understanding of how and why Jesus kept appearing to people after he died. As Jesus' followers began bringing Christ to the OT to help them answer their questions about him, and as later Christians began committing those understandings (along with their understanding of other contemporary traditions about him) to writing, Scripture came to possess a new source of external authority. The OT and burgeoning NT came to receive authority from the creative joining of the reports of Jesus' appearing to people with concomitant theological efforts to thematically present the significance of Jesus' appearing both to contemporaries and posterity.[98]

As interpretations/performances of Scripture began to circulate, they became part of the larger religious culture that, interestingly enough, was already in the business of both receiving and positing Scripture in the first place. As such, the Scriptures were subjected to the prevailing oral and literary conventions of the time. These, in turn, came to influence how Scripture was both culturally received and hermeneutically appropriated in every subsequent re-telling.[99] As J. Dunn and others consistently point out, hermeneutic and performative dimensions of Scripture work together to allow programmatically for a diversity of scriptural traditions, a diversity that fundamentally defines Scripture at its most basic level. Walton and Sandy try to account for this by paying more attention to the dynamic relationship

---

96. See Bovell, "Scriptural Authority and Believing Criticism: The Seriousness of the Evangelical Predicament," *Journal of Philosophy and Scripture* 3 (2005). Online: <http://www.philosophyandscripture.org/Issue3-1/Bovell/Bovell.pdf>.

97. J. Dunn, "The Authority of Scripture according to Scripture (Part 2)," *Churchman* 96 (1982): 202, italics added.

98. Compare A. Farrer's discussion in Farrer, *The Glass of Vision* (Westminster: Dacre, 1948), 38–39.

99. G. Oegema, "On the Contextuality of Translations and the 'Inspiration' of Scriptures," in *Translation of Scripture: Proceedings of a Conference at the Annenberg Research Institute*, May 15–16, 1989, ed. D. Goldenberg (Philadelphia: Annenberg Research Institute, 1990), 112–6.

between the Bible's oral and written aspects.[100] Perhaps another suggestion is to allow the synoptic problem as the biblical paradigm.[101] To understand the "biblical authority" of the gospels, for example, it is imperative that we keep in mind Watson's observation: "Since individual gospels predate the decision that makes them 'canonical' or 'noncanonical,' it should not be assumed that gospels later assigned to the first category originated in isolation from gospels assigned to the second."[102]

When it comes to the Bible's external authority, then, evangelicals should think more seriously about W. Abraham's problematization of the Christian "canon" as criterion.[103] In terms of authority, the Scriptures derive a "canonical" authority only insofar as they can contribute to canonical interpretations of what happened to Jesus, and especially how and why he appeared to people after being crucified.[104] Tabor describes the initial impetus for trying to establish a canonical trajectory: "The messianic candidate comes to the text to inform his or her self-understanding, as well as launch a messianic career, while at the same time external events (e.g., Pilate delivers Jesus to be crucified) elucidate the true meaning of the texts."[105] Tabor makes here a very interesting observation: the authority of Scripture stems from *both* a combination of the ideas presented in them *and* their suitability for understanding contemporary and subsequent historical developments.

What I propose that we do is turn Tabor's observation on its head. Up until the death of Christ, the external authority of Scripture could be

---

100. See J. Walton and B. Sandy, *The Lost World of Scripture: Ancient Literary Culture and Biblical Authority* (Downers Grove, IL: InterVarsity, 2013); compare C. Bovell, *Inerrancy and the Spiritual Formation of Younger Evangelicals* (Eugene, OR: Wipf and Stock, 2007), 103–26.

101. See, for example, J. Dunn, "How the New Testament Began," in *From Biblical Criticism to Biblical Faith: Essays in Honor of Lee Martin McDonald*, ed. W. Brackney and C. Evans (Macon, GA: Mercer University Press, 2007), 122–37.

102. See Watson, *Writing*, 217–8. For one recent proposal, see D. MacDonald, *Two Shipwrecked Gospels: The* Logoi *of Jesus and Papias'* Exposition of Logia *about the Lord* (Atlanta: Society of Biblical Literature, 2012).

103. W. Abraham, *Canon and Criterion in Christian Theology: From the Fathers to Feminism* (New York: Oxford University Press, 1998). Compare Bovell, *By Good and Necessary Consequence*.

104. See also G. Oegema, *Early Judaism and Modern Culture: Literature and Theology* (Grand Rapids: Eerdmans, 2011), 22–24. Compare Stordalen's distinction between "formal" and "actual" canons and especially the roles of each in helping to establish a "canonized interpretation." See T. Stordalen, "The Canonization of Ancient Hebrew and Confucian Literature," *JSOT* 32 (2007): 20–21.

105. J. Tabor, "Are You the One?" 187–8.

attributed to how it was able to elucidate the meaning of specific events (for example, the exile or the destruction of the Temple). Subsequent to Christ's death, however, the external authority of Scripture could be attributed to how Christ's death and, specifically, *his appearing to people*, was able to elucidate the meaning of both the inherited texts and contemporary events. With these developments, the Scriptures came to enjoy a position wherein they became qualified to point people to Jesus: thus, Scripture's external authority.

Even so, A. Farrer had realized long ago that "the martyrdom of a virtuous Rabbi and his miraculous return are not of themselves the redemption of the world."[106] We could paraphrase Farrer's observation by saying, "the external authority of Scripture is not enough to make the Scriptures a means of grace for believers today." For this, we will need to supplement the considerations presented here with a discussion of what "internal" authority the Bible might be said to possess.

---

106. Farrer, *Glass of Vision*, 43.

The Internal Authority of Scripture

Carlos R. Bovell

IN THE PREVIOUS CHAPTER, I briefly explored the idea that Scripture's external authority—what makes the Bible qualified to tell us about Jesus, how he appeared to people after he died, and how best to understand how/why this happened—should be conceived as deriving from the fact that the NT books are the best witnesses available for how early disciples tried to make sense of the fact that Jesus had appeared to people after he had died on a cross. In this chapter, I will take some initial steps toward developing a conception of Scripture's "internal" authority—that feature about our relationship to Scripture that makes Scripture's external authority beside the point—by connecting Scripture's authority to Jesus' continuing activity in "appearing" to believers today.

1. Scripture's "Internal" Authority and the Importance of the Holy Spirit[1]

While the mystical experiences of their authors initially worked "externally" to foster the earliest believers' commitment to gradually receiving the NT writings as Scripture, there is an even more important facet to Scripture's authority that stems from *within* believers. Aside from the social mechanisms of institutional control that became operative in Christian cultures and sub-cultures (which worked to discourage radical breaks from inherited,

---

1. With the title of this section, I do not mean to imply that the Holy Spirit is less important for Scripture's external authority than it is for its internal authority. Compare R. Collins' remark: "[A]lthough it is possible to speak of the Scriptures, the logia of Jesus, and the Twelve as authorities for the Church of New Testament times, ultimately all authority is reducible to that of the Spirit of God who is the authority *par excellence*." Collins, "The Matrix of the NT Canon," *Biblical Theology Bulletin* 7 (1977): 54.

religious traditions), another, and arguably more important, *subjective* component was also at work. What might be called the Bible's "internal" authority derives from the fact that, upon reading Scripture (or hearing Scripture being read), believers find that the Christian Bible is a provision from God to Spirit-filled Christians, which acts as a means of grace for communing with him. By contemplatively reading the Bible and hearing the Bible being read, believers can commune with God "in" the glorified Christ through the Holy Spirit. The Bible exerts its authority upon believers internally by virtue of its being designated by God to serve in a capacity of facilitating communion with God in Christ by the Spirit. Since a disproportionately small percentage of believers have the raw experience of having the resurrected Christ appear to them (much less instruct them),[2] God more regularly coordinates the Spirit in the texts with the Spirit in believers.

The same Spirit that Christians worship and glorify together with the Father and the Son is both the Spirit that resides *within them* and the Spirit that spoke by the prophets. As Novatian wrote in the third century, "The Spirit is not new in the gospel, or even newly given. For it was he himself who accused the people in the prophets, and in the apostles he gave them the appeal to the Gentiles . . . He is therefore one and the same Spirit who was in the prophets and apostles, except that in the former he was present on certain occasions; in the latter he is always present."[3] However, rather than pattern the Bible's inspiration and authority after a *prophetic* model, let us say instead that the internal authority of Scripture is a *functional* one that is provided for by the Holy Spirit. In other words, Scripture's authority is integrally bound to the means it offers believers for communing spiritually with God in Christ by way of the Holy Spirit.[4] The authority of Scripture is exerted "internally" both as the spiritual locus for "the common Christian search" to know the mind of God and in its power to effect the concomitant transformation of the believing community through that communion.[5]

---

2. Compare Kelly: "The singularity of the resurrection event is intensified in that the risen Jesus discloses himself only to privileged witnesses. Christian faith relies on what they once saw, not on what believers now see for themselves." A. Kelly, *The Resurrection Effect: Transforming Christian Life and Thought* (Maryknoll, NY: Orbis, 2008), 16.

3. Cited in J. Elowsky, *We Believe in the Holy Spirit*. Ancient Christian Doctrine 4 (Downers Grove, IL: InterVarsity, 2009), 6.

4. Compare F. Bovon, "Scripture as Promise and a Closure," in *New Testament and Christian Apocrypha*, ed. G. Snyder (Grand Rapids, Baker, 2011), 331.

5. See A. Hunt, *The Inspired Body: Paul, the Corinthians and Divine Inspiration* (Macon, GA: Mercer University Press, 1996), 141–2.

This is, I believe, what Thiselton is referring to when he writes, "To hear the Bible is what it is to be Christian."[6] J. Barr had expressed the same sentiment: "Involvement with the Bible is analytic in being Christian."[7]

With this skeletal, doctrinal framework in place, I will now speculate on how Christ's resurrection gradually came to be acknowledged by the earliest Christians *as* resurrection. The rationale for doing so is to discern whether the "authority" of Christ's resurrection might be appropriated as an analogue to the internal "authority" of Scripture. In what follows, I will not make much of a distinction between the "historical Jesus" and the "Christ of faith," since it was not the historical Jesus who appeared to the disciples or who breathed the Holy Spirit upon them. It was the resurrected Jesus who did this. Not only this, but even the idea that he was resurrected in the first place is a conceptual development that required God's prompting in the earliest disciples' thinking for them to actually entertain it as a serious possibility *with respect to Jesus*.[8] God initiated this through Christ's post-Easter appearances.

2. The Resurrection as Pivotal, But Already Part of Creation

J. Moore recounts that at the first Oxford "Remembering for the Future" conference, held in 1988, H. Maccoby quipped in his opening remarks that "Jews would have little problem with Christians and Jesus in particular if

---

6. A. Thiselton, *Life after Death: A New Approach to the Last Things* (Grand Rapids: Eerdmans, 2012), 52. Thiselton stresses that we "respect the special status of the Bible or hearing God's voice through it, without in the least neglecting the 'human' side" (52).

7. Cited by Thiselton, *Life*, 52. Compare T. W. Isherwood, "The Authority of Scripture," *Churchman* 58 (1944): 4: "It would seem, therefore, that the Authority of Scripture is inextricably bound up with essential Christian experience, and that only by denying the latter can we escape from the challenge of the former."

8. Cranfield seems to have argued that the *conceptual tools* were not available to the disciples for them to make such a connection in the first place: "[B]efore the event, neither the women nor the disciples had the slightest expectation of their Master's being raised from the dead before the general eschatological resurrection." C. Cranfield, "The Resurrection of Jesus Christ," *ExpTim* 101 (1990): 170. However, the angelology of the DSS argues against Cranfield's reasons for why the disciples were so slow to apply a resurrection to Jesus. Compare P. Perkins, "The Resurrection of Jesus of Nazareth," in *Studying the Historical Jesus: Evaluations of the State of Current Research*, ed. C. Evans (New York: Brill, 1994), 426–34.

Christians would just give up the resurrection."[9] The understanding that "resurrection" occurred *and that it happened to Christ* is distinctive to a Christian view of God and his creation. The Christian Gospels all converge on the determination that the best way to express what happened to Jesus is to say he was resurrected.[10] Thus, it is widely recognized that Christianity has an eminently historical component; however, this is not to say that the *authority of its Scriptures* is commensurate with their historicity.[11] The

---

9. See Moore, "The Amazing Mr. Jesus," *Shofar* 28 (2010): 34–35. A. Kelly observes how the resurrection poses a serious problem for interreligious dialogue: "[I]n the sphere of interfaith dialogue when theology searches for points of contact with the great spiritualities of the world, the resurrection so intensifies the particularity of Christ that it might be best left unmentioned." Kelly, "Making the Resurrection Reasonable—Or Reason 'Resurrectional'?" in *Christianity and Secular Reason: Classical Themes and Modern Developments* (Notre Dame, IN: University of Notre Dame Press, 2012), 191.

10. H. Frei put it this way: "[The believer] would have to affirm that the New Testament authors were right in insisting that it is more nearly correct to think of Jesus as factually raised, bodily if you will, than not to think of him in this manner. (But the qualification "more nearly . . . than not" is important in order to guard against speculative explanations of the resurrection from theories of immortality, possibilities of visionary or auditory experiences, possibilities of resuscitating dead bodies, miracles in general, etc.)." Regarding the Apostle's Creed, Marxsen wrote: "It seems to me important to draw attention to the fact that the very wording of this article shows that the individual statements are not made because we believe or ought to believe in *them* but because they describe *the being* in whom we believe." Frei, *Identity of Jesus Christ*, 144; W. Marxsen, *The Resurrection of Jesus of Nazareth* (Philadelphia: Fortress, 1970), 32.

11. Some evangelical scholars are all too happy to discover ("miraculously") that critical tools overwhelmingly authenticate the Gospels' historicity. See Amy-Jill Levine, "Christian Faith and the Study of the Historical Jesus: A Response to Bock, Keener, and Webb," *Journal for the Study of the Historical Jesus* 9 (2011): 97. Compare Miller: "Bock's essay is a fine example of how evangelicals can use traditional historical-Jesus criteria to further their project of authenticating the Gospels. But I assume—although I would be happy to be corrected—that evangelical scholars do not allow those same criteria to lead to negative historical conclusions, i.e., to the judgment that passages are non-historical fictions." See R. J. Miller, "When It's Futile to Argue about the Historical Jesus: A Response to Bock, Keener, and Webb," *Journal for the study of the Historical Jesus* 9 (2011): 88–89. R. Webb is optimistic that there can still be a mediating position that would allow evangelicals to do critical history; Keener agrees with Webb. See R. Webb, "Methodological Naturalism: Engaging the Responses of Robert J. Miller and Amy-Jill Levine," *Journal for the Study of the Historical Jesus* 9 (2011): 118–23; and C. Keener, "A Brief Reply to Robert Miller and Amy-Jill Levine," *Journal for the Study of the Historical* Jesus 9 (2011): 114. Keener is right to insist on a wide spectrum of evangelical thought. Even so, I think Fairbairn is more or less accurate in his description of what evangelical scholars hope to accomplish *programmatically* when they engage in biblical studies: "We are trying to show the liberal academy that even if one adopts its standards for historicity, even if one uses its tools of interpretation, the Bible still shines forth as an accurate, reliable set

Christian claim is not to historical data, nor even the Scriptures that contain it; rather, it is to a divine revelation received, formulated, and disseminated by Jesus' earliest followers in response to his appearing to them after he died. Scripture is a product of that revelation, but it is not the revelation itself. In many ways, the Scriptures are one step (or more likely, several steps) removed from being *that* kind of reflection. Perhaps evangelical apologetics has been trying too hard to tie Scripture to history in order to compensate for Lessing's "ditch," the gap that stands between contemporary believers and the Easter events.

Connected to this, evangelical apologists have concentrated their efforts on proving the historicity of the resurrection itself in their defense of the Christian faith. For my part, I find it helpful to keep in mind that, to say that the resurrection "happened to Jesus" is not necessarily to say that it happened to him "historically." I think O'Collins' instinct is right to protest against the majority view: "the resurrection is not an event *in* space and time and hence should not be called historical [since t]hrough the resurrection, Christ . . . moves outside the world and its history, outside the ordinary datable, localizable conditions of our experience—to become an 'otherworldly' reality."[12] It will be my contention below that we ought not conceive of Christ's resurrection as the basis for a future resurrection of humans. In my own view, it is much more fruitful to think of an ongoing resurrection of humans that is already taking place—*that Christ participated in and transformed by participating in it*—which serves as the basis for Christ's resurrection.[13] What Christ's life, death, resurrection, and ascension accomplished was a transformation of the resurrection—again, a process already in place before Christ was born—into an eternal, spiritual glorification that allows for our participation in God's divinity in absolute communion through the Son and the Spirit.

The privilege of being a Christian believer is to be found, I submit, in enjoying the preliminary phases of divine communion, participation, and transformation *in this life* (albeit in miniature) through prayer, the

---

of documents. In short, we are trying to engage in scholarly level apologetics, to fight a battle on our opponents' turf and still win the battle." D. Fairbairn, "Patristic Exegesis and Theology: The Cart and the Horse," *Westminster Theological Journal* 69 (2007): 18.

12. G. O'Collins, "Is the Resurrection an 'Historical' Event?" *Heythrop Journal* 8 (1967): 384.

13. Compare C. Bowen, *The Resurrection in the New Testament: An Examination of the Earliest References to the Rising of Jesus and of Christians from the Dead* (New York: G. P. Putnam's Sons, 1911), 65–66.

churches' liturgy, personal and communal worship, public and private readings of Scripture, hearing the Scriptures being read, Christian fellowship, etc. In other words, by virtue of Jesus' resurrection and ascension (with Jesus being the "first fruit," as it were), each of the several facets of Christian spirituality is put to the service of preparation for the life to come. A spiritual benefit accrues to Christians, so to speak, to the effect that "we are God's children now; what we will be has not yet been revealed. What we do know is this: when he is revealed, we will be like him, for we will see him as he is" (1 John 3:2). It is precisely this spiritual matrix of communion, participation, transformation, and preparation that Christians should be thinking about whenever they reflect upon and speak of Scripture's contemporary "authority." Indeed, is this not what *the* foundational text for evangelical bibliology actually suggests (2 Tim 3:16)? The role, then, that Scripture plays will involve "teaching," "reproof," "correction," and "training in righteousness"—all of this in the service of "everyone who belongs to God" so they can be made "proficient, equipped for every good work" (2 Tim 3:16–17).

3. Mary's Experience as Paradigm for Seeing the Resurrected Lord

In John 20:11–16, the fourth evangelist describes an extraordinary scene:

> But Mary stood weeping outside the tomb. As she wept, she bent over to look into the tomb; and she saw two angels in white, sitting where the body of Jesus had been lying, one at the head and the other at the feet. They said to her, "Woman, why are you weeping?" She said to them, "They have taken away my Lord, and I do not know where they have laid him." When she had said this, she turned round and saw Jesus standing there, but she did not know that it was Jesus. Jesus said to her, "Woman, why are you weeping? For whom are you looking?" Supposing him to be the gardener, she said to him, "Sir, if you have carried him away, tell me where you have laid him, and I will take him away." Jesus said to her, "Mary!" She turned and said to him in Hebrew, "Rabbouni!" (which means Teacher). Jesus said to her, "Do not hold on to me, because I have not yet ascended to the Father. But go to my brothers and say to them, 'I am ascending to my Father and your Father, to my God and your God.'"

What an exciting passage! Traditionally, as students of the text we might ask, "When and where is this meeting thought to be taking place?" "Outside the tomb" seems a sensible answer, but perhaps we can get more out of this pericope if we do not suppose at the outset that the story is aiming to provide a straightforward, publicly accessible account of what "really" happened.[14] I would argue that we should read the passage instead as reporting Mary's encounter with the risen Christ that occurred, not in historical but in transcendent space, a vision experience wherein she interacted both with angels and with Jesus. In fact, it seems more to the point of the fourth Gospel that its account of the gospel story is instructing readers *how to understand* what happened after Jesus' death. In other words, not one of the Gospel writers is interested in giving us details about a resurrection.[15] The evangelists' primary purpose is to standardize a distinctly "Christian" interpretation for how most fruitfully to understand the post-Easter events, namely, *that Christ appeared to his disciples after being crucified.*[16]

Some evangelicals see the suggestion that portions of the gospels ought not to be taken historically as a very serious threat to the integrity of the faith. These evangelicals take an "all-or-nothing" stance, fearing that if any one passage is taken metaphorically then they all will be, or at least,

---

14. Compare G. Williams who explores the "narrative space" of the tomb created by the evangelist in the Gospel of Mark. See Williams, "Narrative Space, Angelic Revelation, and the End of Mark's Gospel," *Journal for the Study of the New Testament* (2013): 263–84.

15. One will look in vain for a description of the resurrection.

16. I think this is also the key to approaching Gen 1–4. The creation accounts do not reveal what happened at creation, but what believers should take away from the fact that there *is* a creation. The biblical accounts may provide the beginnings of a conceptual framework that churches might work with, but the matter becomes complicated rather quickly since the bulk of Scripture's "meaning" is ultimately supplied by the Bible's interpreters, especially in today's post-critical environment where we self-consciously learn from history, science, and culture how more fruitfully to engage the biblical materials. See here N. M. Wilders, *The Theologian and His Universe: Theology and Cosmology from the Middle Ages to the Present* (New York: Seabury, 1982).

Schoedel describes a similar line of thinking in Irenaeus: "Thus we can say 'that' God brought forth matter, but we do not know 'whence' or 'how' he did so. Such inquiries only lead to 'making infinite conjectures' and should be left to God." In the contemporary context, it seems prudent for Christians to say that the Bible has nothing at all to tell us about *how* God created, only *that* God created. See W. Schoedel, "Theological Method in Irenaeus ('Adversus Haereses'. 2. 25–8)," *Journal of Theological Studies* 35 (1984): 27. Regarding Christ's ascension specifically, Donne remarks: "[T]he *meaning* of the Ascension is of far greater importance than the manner of our Lord's final departure from this world." B. Donne, *Christ Ascended: The Significance of the Ascension in the New Testament* (Exeter: Paternoster, 1983), 7.

nothing would then prohibit reading entire Gospels metaphorically.[17] To allay their fears of a potential "slippery slope," they have devised a system where only an unambiguous cue in a gospel text can warrant metaphorical reading. A recent example involves NT apologist M. Licona's proposal that the "harrowing of hell" pericope in Mat 27:52–53 be taken "poetically." The controversy that ensued ended up costing him both of his jobs. Geisler, one of Licona's chief "prosecutors," argued that to read these words as anything other than historical would open the door to dismissing other passages besides. He warned in an open letter to Licona that, "neither is there any indication in the text that a historical understanding of the resurrection of the saints should be excluded from the text." Geisler and those who agree with him do not want the Bible's interpreters deciding what portions are historical and what portions are not in ways that might undercut their apologetic work in support of the Bible's historical reliability.[18]

I do not feel the same burden when reading the gospel stories. Still, perhaps others may, and so, in support of my suggestion that Mary's interaction with the angels and with Jesus occurred in a vision and not publicly as part of "history," consider also Luke 24:23 where it is said that a group of women had a "vision of angels" at the tomb. Such language suggests that we should consider the possibility that the accounts of the women encountering Jesus after his death are to be read in a different way. And indeed, is there not in this story about Mary a sense that with the departure of the two disciples, the setting has become surreal?[19] Why does this place (outside the tomb, wherever it is supposed to be) suddenly take on features of a mythical, narratival "space" where heaven and earth so conspicuously overlap (e.g., occupying "transcendent" time, describing a place where angels openly interact with humans)?[20] The setting becomes a sacred space, part

---

17. See, for example, J. Crossan, *The Power of Parable: How Fiction by Jesus Became Fiction about Jesus* (New York: HarperOne, 2012).

18. See Licona, *The Resurrection of Jesus: A New Historiographical Approach* (Downers Grove, IL: InterVarsity, 2010), 553; and N. Geisler, "An Open Letter to Mike Licona on His View of the Resurrected Saints in Matthew 27:52–53," online: < http://normangeisler.net/articles/Bible/Inspiration-Inerrancy/Licona/1stOpenLetterToMikeLicona.htm >. Similarly, in 1982, Geisler was instrumental in stirring the controversy surrounding R. Gundry's application of redaction criticism on Matthew's nativity story.

19. Compare Zwiep's questioning of Luke: "Since the resurrection of Jesus is never presented in the NT, as a return to his physical, terrestrial life as e.g. in the case of Lazarus, the question arises, from where does Jesus appear to his disciples." See, A. W. Zwiep, *The Ascension of the Messiah in Lukan Christology* (New York: Brill, 1997), 28.

20. Cranfield observes: "The presence of an angel or angels in the Gospel Easter

of a literary juxtaposition between the temple in Jerusalem and its counterpart in heaven. Further, there may also be an allusion here to God's holy mountain, a thematic association with God's holy temple.[21]

The pericope raises another important question: *who* would have the privilege of entering such sacred space? It may come as something of a surprise, therefore, that the fourth evangelist presents Mary Magdalene as *the only one* present in this scene; the other two disciples have, by now, fled from the tomb. This makes Mary Magdalene one of the most significant figures in the Gospel story.[22] O'Collins and Kendall do not exaggerate when they write, "Mary Magdalene is the human figure who holds the events together."[23] She is presented as the first to find the tomb empty on her earlier visit to the tomb to weep there.[24] Her story of visiting the tomb stands

---

narratives is probably for a good many people an additional reason for doubting the truth of the Resurrection." Stump writes: "Whether accounts without angels are more historical than accounts giving a role to angels depends on whether reality includes angels or not." It would seem also to depend on what part of "reality" angels occupy and whether that part of reality should count as "historical." To be clear, I am not suggesting that an Easter angel makes for "a legendary accretion" or that the presence of angels should cause us to "[r]eject the truth of the resurrection itself." I am simply suggesting that drawing attention to the fact that the nature of what Mary was experiencing most likely involved an altered state of consciousness. See Cranfield, "Resurrection," 168–9; and E. Stump, "Visits to the Sepulcher and Biblical Exegesis," *Faith and Philosophy* 6 (1989): 37 n19.

21. And there are further mythic allusions to the king's palace or royal garden. Thus, Mary thought that Jesus was the gardener. See N. Wyatt, "'Supposing Him to Be a Gardener' (John 20, 15): A Study of the Paradise Motif in John," *ZNW* 81 (1990): 21–38. The Ark of the Covenant in the holy of holies is another association readers might make with this otherworldly scene of two angels positioned on either side of where Jesus had been laid. See R. Smith, *Easter Gospels*, 161, cited in C. Osiek, "The Women at the Tomb: What Are They Doing There?" *Ex Auditu* 9 (1993): 101.

22. For my part, I am amazed I had not recognized this until recently when re-reading the fourth Gospel multiple times during a short period of study. Apparently, Mary's singular role in the fourth Gospel is often overlooked. It stands to reason that, based on this scene from the Gospel of John, Mary Magdalene would have become a figure of great renown within the early Christian movements. I understand, for example, why an "apocryphal" *Gospel of Mary* would have gone into circulation and why Esther A. de Boer might propose that Mary is the fourth Gospel's "beloved disciple," the author of the Gospel. See de Boer, "Mary Magdalene and the Disciple Jesus Loved," and Marjanen, "Mary Magdalene, A Beloved Disciple."

23. G. O'Collins and D. Kendall, "Mary Magdalene as Major Witness to Jesus' Resurrection," *Theological Studies* 48 (1987): 645.

24. Interestingly enough, Osiek wonders whether the fourth evangelist's account turns out to be the *most* historical since John is the "most forthright and least threatened by women's presence, for Mary Magdalene is just there, weeping." Osiek, "Women," 103.

in counterpoint to that of Mary of Bethany's visit to the tomb of Lazarus. In the Lazarus story (John 12:1–11), Mary of Bethany went to the tomb in order to see Jesus, but the crowds assumed that she was going there to weep; in the present scene, Mary Magdalene really does visit the tomb in order to weep, but instead she sees Jesus.[25] It is no coincidence that both stories climax in resurrection.[26]

In Lazarus' case, people came to Bethany to see Lazarus with the result that they got to see publicly the one who had been resurrected. In Jesus' case, however, when people (i.e., his disciples) came to see the one who had been resurrected, they did *not* get to see him. Indeed, they could not see him publicly—they were not yet shown in what way they would be able to see him—that is, not until he revealed himself to them and made himself known. Notice that the empty tomb plays virtually no role in the disciples' coming to believe the resurrection. The fourth evangelist states unequivocally that the disciples failed to see any significance in Mary's finding the tomb empty: "For as yet they did not understand the Scripture, that he must rise from the dead" (John 20:9). Perhaps the answer to Judas' question—"Lord, how is it that you will reveal yourself to us, and not to the world?" (John 14:22)—instructs us as to the manner of resurrection Jesus actually experienced and to the manner of "seeing" that is required in order to see the Lord.

---

25. Compare with connections made in I. Rosa Kitzberger, "Mary of Bethany and Mary of Magdala—Two Female Characters in the Johannine Passion Narrative: A Feminist, Narrative-Critical Reader-Response," *New Testament Studies* 41 (1995): 580–84. E. Schweizer also follows a similar sort of progression *from* the appearance of Jesus to Mary *back to* the interaction of Jesus with Martha and Mary just before the raising of Lazarus. He explains: "There is a section of the fourth gospel which became more and more important for my thinking [about the resurrection]. It is the dialogue between Martha and Jesus in the story of the resurrection of Lazarus in chapter 11:23–8." Schweizer, "Resurrection—Fact or Illusion?" *Horizons in Biblical Theology* 1 (1979): 151.

26. Dunn observes that the Johannine motifs in the Lazarus story "overwhelm the parallels," so much so that "[t]here would appear to be a danger here of Johannine elaboration becoming detached from its historical roots and of uncomfortable precedents being set." J. Dunn, "John and the Oral Gospel Tradition," in *Jesus and the Oral Gospel Tradition*, ed. H. Wansborough (New York: Sheffield, 1991), 375. In other words, a historical miracle involving Jesus raising a person from the dead is elaborated upon by the fourth evangelist for the very purpose of illuminating the significance of Jesus' resurrection for his hearers/readers.

4. Seeing the Resurrected Lord Tantamount to Seeing God

In the fourth Gospel, Peter and the other disciple come to the tomb only after Mary tells them about finding it empty. After inspecting the empty tomb for themselves, the two disciples unceremoniously leave. Mary Magdalene remains alone, presumably to mourn, but while there, she sees a vision of angels and hears their announcement. Her choice to remain at the tomb leads to Jesus appearing to her. With this vision, Mary Magdalene becomes the first to understand that Jesus is somehow alive. John 20:9 and our present pericope make the implication clear: the fact that Jesus was "raised from the dead" is not something that a person would have concluded by their own powers of deduction. A special dispensation of the Spirit is required for the realization that a "resurrection" took place.

Through the narratival framework of the Johannine material, the fourth evangelist presents Mary as the recipient of a mystical, religious experience—a privileged, Spirit-induced vision that allows her to: 1) learn that Jesus was not dead; 2) understand that Jesus had been resurrected and is about to ascend to his father; and 3) piece together that Jesus' resurrection had immediate ramifications for Jesus' followers and for the shape that Jesus' ministry would begin to take through them.[27] As a result of this vision, it had been revealed to Mary that 1) though Jesus had died, it is still possible to commune with him; 2) one could commune with God the Father *through* the risen Jesus; and 3) to commune with the risen Christ is, in fact, to commune with God.[28] The Johannine logic of the fourth Gospel prepared readers for this final conclusion all the way back in John 1: since Mary was the first to see the risen Lord, *she was also the first to see God.*[29]

---

27. What Williams says about the women at the tomb in Mark is true of Mary Magdalene here; they were active recipients of revelation: "If we see this as a revelatory episode described in a striking and yet well-thought-out setting (i.e. the tomb), with carefully drawn angelic conventions, then the weight of the communication to the women emerges clearly. The resurrection is revealed to *them*; they receive a prophetic commission to bring out the Gospel." See Williams, "Narrative Space," 279.

28. One tradition presents Mary as knowing more than even the Twelve on account of her paradigmatic vision of the risen Jesus. See E. de Boer, *The Gospel of Mary: Beyond a Gnostic and Biblical Mary Magdalene* (Continuum, 2005), 194.

29. Compare W. Meeks, "Equal to God," in *The Conversation Continues: Studies in Paul and John in Honor of J. Louis Martyn*, ed. R. Fortna and B. Gaventa (Nashville: Abingdon, 1990), 318-9.

The Internal Authority of Scripture

Toward the beginning of the fourth Gospel, in John 1:51, readers are indirectly told by Jesus that by the time they reach the end of this Johannine re-telling of the "Life and Acts of Jesus,"[30] they will have seen angels ascending and descending on the Son of Man.[31] This serves as an invitation for readers of the Gospel to keep reading in order that, by the time they finish, they may come to see God. I propose that this Johannine invitation reflects in miniature what "internal" authority the entire NT has for believers. My claim is that the authority of the NT lies in the fact that, by virtue of attentively reading and/or hearing the NT Scriptures being read, believers are given repeated opportunities to spiritually commune with God.[32] Describing the authority of the fourth Gospel, W. Meeks explains, "*The book functions for its readers in precisely the same way that epiphany of its hero functions within its narratives and dialogues.*"[33] My suggestion is that, by extension, the entire NT is a spiritual epiphany of God centered on the reality of Christ. It is made manifest in the hearts of Christian believers through the Holy Spirit, the Spirit of Christ which they possess. The Bible is in every way a historical and cultural artifact, yet it is also an anagogical *product of the Church* endowed with the Holy Spirit *in service of the Church*, providing a sacred space, as it were, where Christians can have communion with God and the risen Christ through the Holy Spirit.

Commenting on the exegetical implications of John 1:51, Neyrey explains that "[n]ot just Nathanael, but all the disciples are promised a vision like Jacob's vision."[34] What kind of vision was Jacob thought to have had? To answer this, we should not look to the OT directly but rather to how the

---

30. Compare G. Nicholson, *Death as Departure: The Johannine Descent-Ascent Schema* (Chico, CA: Scholars, 1983), 30.

31. I understand a "gospel" to be a telling of the life and acts of Jesus. It is admittedly difficult to define "gospel," yet perhaps we can do no better than say that it is "a text which purports to give information about the life and teaching of Jesus," which is to include, in Jesus' case, acts and teachings delivered *after* his resurrection. See A. Gregory and C. Tuckett, "Series Preface," in *The Gospel of Mary* (New York: Oxford University Press, 2007), vi.

32. This is one reason why Christians cannot help but appeal to Scripture when trying to give an account for its authority. Evangelicals, however, like to emphasize Scripture's *statements*. It would be better, I would argue, to place the emphasis on its *use* and its transformative capacity.

33. W. Meeks, "The Man from Heaven in Johannine Sectarianism," *Journal of Biblical Literature* 91 (1972): 69.

34. J. Neyrey, "The Jacob Allusions in John 1:51," *Catholic Biblical Quarterly* 44 (1982): 589.

OT was being read at the time that this Gospel was written. As Rowland explains, "the author of the fourth Gospel was not dealing merely with the Bible as we have it but also with a long tradition of scriptural interpretation which had considerable influence on the way in which the original texts were understood."[35] Agreeing with Quispel, Kanagaraj states that John 1:51 is a midrashic promise for "the vision of the glorified Christ," a "vision" of God's glory comparable to those known from early Merkabah traditions.[36] Following Schwarz, Meeks sees a "form of solemn prophecy" in John 1:51 that "demands some fulfillment in the subsequent narrative."[37]

5. Mystical Experience, the idea of heavenly ascent, and reading Scripture

Toward the beginning of the fourth Gospel, the claim is made that no one has ever seen God (John 1:18), a bold assertion that, although other figures are known through tradition to have travelled to heaven and seen God, the fact of the matter is that those taking such journeys were only able to do so while still being kept at a considerable distance from God. The fourth evangelist's claim, by contrast, is that, comparatively speaking, Jesus Christ is the only one about whom it can be said that he has gone to heaven and seen God. To wit, his ascension is on a different order when compared to the rest, for Jesus Christ did not ascend *so that* he could see God. Rather, Jesus ascended because he first had come down from heaven and was only now returning. His ascension is precisely a *return* to heaven. Of no one else can such a claim be made. The Johannine Gospel is presented as "a form of mystagogy," containing some elements of apocalyptic, but even more

---

35. C. Rowland, "John 1.51, Jewish Apocalyptic and Targumic Tradition," *NTS* 30 (1984): 500. Sidebottom saw a problem with Odeberg's early connections between the merkabah and John 1:51, but Rowland explains: "The fact that the ascent preceded the descent is explained by angels returning from earth to heaven to impart the information about Jacob to other angels who then descend to gaze at the features of the patriarch" (503). Neyrey

suggests an alternate solution: "[t]he angels, moreover, first ascend and then descend; they are already in heaven and ascend more intimately into heaven, even toward the heavenly throne." See Neyrey, "Jacob Allusions," 597–8.

36. J. Kanagarag, "Jesus the King, Merkabah Mysticism and the Gospel of John," *Tyndale Bulletin* 47 (1996): 351–2.

37. Meeks, "Man from Heaven," 51.

elements of mysticism. Rowland goes so far as to say that the fourth Gospel is "an apocalypse in reverse."[38]

Early Merkabah traditions were fascinated with the theophanies presented in scriptural passages such as Ex 19 and Ezek 1.[39] Ezekiel's throne vision in particular inspired later Jewish mystics to practice rituals and recite prayers in preparation for visions, hoping to catch a glimpse of God seated upon his heavenly throne.[40] To what extent mystical practices comprised an integral part of Jewish religious culture during the Second Temple period is not yet clear.[41] Extant documents show that, at least by the second century CE, neighboring cultures in antiquity (the Greeks, for example) had developed an interest in learning how to "act upon" the gods. The *Chaldean Oracles* is one of the earliest evidences among the Greeks for the "creation of a ritual to achieve ascent of the soul while the individual was still alive."[42]

Even so, recent scholarship has been reluctant to view early Christian mysticism as being primarily influenced by magical rites associated with

---

38. C. Rowland and C. R. A. Morray-Jones, *The Mystery of God: Early Jewish Mysticism and the New Testament* (Leiden: Brill, 2009), 130, 131.

39. Ezekiel's vision was apparently the first of its kind. See G. Quispel, "Ezekiel 1.26 in Jewish Mysticism and Gnosis," *Vigiliae Christianae* 34 (1980): 1–13.

40. R. Lesses, *Ritual Practices to Gain Power: Angels, Incantations, and Revelation in Early Jewish Mysticism* (Harrisburg, PA: Trinity International, 1998).

41. In his section on mysticism, F. E. Peters writes that this sort of Jewish mysticism began with Rabbi Akiba in the early second century C. E. See Peters, *The Monotheists: Jews, Christians and Muslims in Conflict and Competition, Volume 2: The Words and Will of God* (Princeton, NJ: Princeton University Press, 2003), 296–7. In an important article, J. W. Bowker draws attention to Rabbi Johanan ben Zakkai in the first century C. E. See Bowker, "'Merkabah' Vision and the Visions of Paul," *Journal of Semitic Studies* 16 (1971): 157. For the earliest mention of Merkabah in the rabbinic literature, see D. Halperin, *The Faces of the Chariot: Early Jewish Responses to Ezekiel's Vision* (Tübingen: Mohr, 1988), 11–37, and his comprehensive *The Merkabah in Rabbinic Literature* (New Haven: American Oriental Society, 1980). A. Lieber suggests that perhaps a communal, mystical experience stands behind the Qumranic "Songs of the Sabbath Sacrifice." (I will revisit this idea in a later section of this chapter.) See Lieber, "Voice and Vision: Song as a Vehicle for Ecstatic Experience in *Songs of the Sabbath Sacrifice*," in *Of Scribes and Sages: Early Jewish Interpretation and Transmission of Scripture; Volume 2: Later Versions and Traditions*, ed. C. Evans (New York: T & T Clark, 2004), 51–58.

42. See S. Johnston, "Rising to the Occasion: Theurgic Ascent in Its Cultural Milieu," in *Envisioning Magic: A Princeton Seminar and Symposium*, ed. P. Schäfer and H. Kippenberg (New York, Brill, 1997), 166. According to R. Majercik, "the *Oracles* were regarded by the later Neoplatonists—from Porphyry (c. 232–303 C.E.) to Damasius (c. 462–537 C.E.)—as authoritative revelatory literature equal in importance only to Plato's *Timaeus*." See R. Majercik, *The Chaldean Oracles: Text, Translation, and Commentary* (New York: Brill, 1989), 2.

Greek mystery religions.[43] With the widespread acceptance of a fundamentally Jewish context for the emergence of Christianity, there has been less motivation to look outside of Second Temple Judaic culture for help with understanding the earliest Christians' perception of their religion. Accordingly, recent efforts have focused on determining to what extent the Jewish religion of the Second Temple period was typified by mysticism. How similar, for example, might earlier strands of Jewish religious expression be to the later mystical strands associated with rabbinic Judaism?[44] Might the ancient apocalypses testify to mystical experiences Jewish seers actually had, or is "apocalypse" merely a literary genre created in response to specific social and political developments?[45] According to J. Dan, "there is no doubt that there is a strong link" between Greek magic and the magical aspects depicted in the later hekhalot literature, but the mysticism evidenced so far by the DSS appears to have been more *exegetical* than it was magical.[46]

When studying the DSS, for example, a student can purchase a volume devoted to "mystical" texts and another still that focuses on "exegetical" texts. It is worth asking, however, whether exegetical texts are—*on account of their being exegetical*— unable to also be considered mystical. Was there an overarching mystical context for the reading, recital, and performance of sacred texts? Certain OT Scriptures might well have been read *mystically*

---

43. E. R. Dodds thought that even the relationship between Greek mystery religions and Neoplatonist philosophical schools to be rather limited. See Dodds, "Theurgy and Its Relationship to Neoplatonism," *Journal of Roman Studies* 37 (1947): 55–69.

44. In his pioneering work, G. Scholem tried to date some of the hekhalot hymns as early as he could and argue for continuity between earliest strands of rabbinic mysticism and the later hekhalot literature. In one lecture, though, he admitted that the (then) newly discovered Nag-Hammadi library and the Dead Sea Scrolls were going to revolutionize scholarship and that it would be interesting to see whether, once studied, they would lend support to his position. See, for example, Scholem, *Major Trends in Jewish Mysticism* (New York: Shocken, 1946); and Scholem, *Jewish Gnosticism, Merkabah Mysticism, and Talmudic Tradition* (New York: Jewish Theological Seminary of America, 1965).

45. When proposing a definition for "apocalypse," J. Collins cautions that, "while a complete study of a genre must consider function and social setting, neither of these factors can determine the definition. At least in the case of ancient literature our knowledge of function and setting is often extremely hypothetical and cannot provide a firm basis for generic classification." Collins defines "apocalypse" as "a genre of revelatory literature with a narrative framework, in which a revelation is mediated by an otherworldly being to a human recipient, disclosing a transcendent reality which is both temporal, insofar as it envisages eschatological salvation, and spatial insofar as it involves another, supernatural world." Collins, "Apocalypse: The Morphology of a Genre," *Semeia* 14 (1979): 2, 9.

46. J. Dan, *The Ancient Jewish Mysticism* (Tel Aviv: MOD Books, 1993), 221.

The Internal Authority of Scripture

during the time of Christ. Might it be that some within Second Temple Judaism were trained to read psalms, for example, in ways that led to mystical experiences to gain a vision of heaven and/or God? It is very likely that *some* read Scriptures seeking to make sense of mystical experiences they had already had.[47]

It seems to me perfectly reasonable to suppose that Jesus himself came from an environment that accepted and promoted the validity of mystical experiences. For example, both Joseph and Zechariah (Jesus' father and uncle respectively) are presented in the gospels as mystics, as persons in the habit of having dreams and visions that involved revelation by means of angels. B. Chilton suggests that John the Baptist likely taught Jesus how to meditate on the first chapter of Ezekiel, for example, in order to precipitate mystical experiences. Chilton further proposes that, since John's followers, including Jesus, were illiterate, they would have committed the Scripture to memory and then meditated upon it. Chilton observes:

> "Look at what you listen to!" Jesus told his own disciples later in his life (Mark 4:24), a technique he had learned from John. The words themselves were viewed as sacred, imbued with divine force. Without the correct intonation, they would lack the energy needed to transport the initiate to the locus of God's presence.... As Jesus mastered the techniques of envisioning the Chariot, John began to teach him of God's Spirit, which flowed from the Chariot to all creation.[48]

So exegesis could be mystical and mysticism can be exegetical. I propose that the numinous experiences that accompany the reading of Scripture, along with the anagogical contemplation of its stories, images, motifs, and teachings, together constitute the *internal* authority of Scripture.

It seems unfortunate that evangelicals should so frequently overlook the subjective, anagogical facet of scriptural reading. When evangelicals place the emphasis on a "high" regard for Scripture, it becomes only natural for them to take *their* understanding of how exegesis should be done— which often tends to view exegesis simply as a method for extracting

---

47. Crump is most certainly right: "It is the experience of Christ himself that produces the church." What Crump is saying is that it was *their experience of Christ* that caused the early church to read and interpret Scripture in the ways they did. See D. Crump, *Encountering Jesus, Encountering Scripture: Reading the Bible Critically in* Faith (Grand Rapids: Eerdmans, 2013), 39.

48. Chilton, *Rabbi Jesus: An Intimate Biography* (New York: Doubleday, 2000), 52–53.

information from Scripture—and conflate that with what the Qumran exegetes, for example, must have been doing when they read Scripture. Or else, because evangelicals hold grammatico-historical approaches to exegesis as the standard by which all interpretations should be measured, they could not help but apply the same criteria to the exegetes at Qumran. By that standard, they found the techniques exhibited at Qumran (which, in very important ways, appear to be very similar to the way the NT writers interpreted their Scriptures) lacking, prompting questions as to whether such approaches even can or should be carried out by believers today. A consideration that I do not think has received the attention it deserves is this: what if the exegetical endeavor at Qumran functioned primarily, not as a way of obtaining information from Scripture, but rather, as a disciplined way to *see* God by virtue of mystical experiences?[49]

What I am suggesting is that perhaps exegesis was not merely a way to extract information pertinent to faith, but more importantly, a way of experiencing or "seeing" God. In other words, the internal authority that Scripture possesses should not be measured by the "true" propositions that it contains, but rather, in the way that the Spirit in Scripture cries out, as it were, to the Spirit within us and allows us to commune with God mystically, to "see" him in the Spirit. The apocalyptic literature of Second Temple Judaism gives testimony to the fact that it was known that people could meditate on Scripture and, by virtue of mystical experiences, see God while in an altered state of consciousness.

6. Heavenly Journeys and the authority of Scripture

Himmelfarb distinguishes the early Jewish apocalypses from later, mystical texts by observing that "apocalypses never offer advice about how to imitate the protagonist in his ascent. Even if the experience of the author or of someone known to the author stands behind the accounts, there is no attempt to explain how to achieve the experience."[50] R. Lesses emphasizes

---

49. Compare Alexander: "Religious experience does not happen in a vacuum . . . The exegesis of tradition can provoke new religious experience, especially if tradition is read intensely and reverently in an act of *lectio divina*." P. Alexander, *Mystical Texts* (New York: T & T Clark, 2006), 95.

50. M. Himmelfarb, "Heavenly Ascent and the Relationship of the Apocalypse and the Hekhalot Literature," *Hebrew Union College Annual* 59 (1988): 100.

the same point when comparing Jewish and Christian apocalypses with their Mediterranean counterparts:

> Among Jews and Christians, the extensive apocalyptic tradition describes ascents to heaven or visions of heaven (for example, the *Enoch* literature, the *Apocalypse of Abraham*, *3 Baruch*, the Revelation of John, and the *Ascension of Isaiah*). Angels also descend to earth to bring humans up to heaven or reveal secrets to them (for example, *1 Enoch* 7 and 8), but in this literature, human beings do not compel them to descend. On the contrary, neither the heavenward ascent of a person nor the descent from heaven by a divine being come about through human volition.[51]

Dean-Otting concurs, noting that in the early Jewish apocalypses "[t]he theurgic, magical practices of the later mystical ascents found in the Hekaloth literature are entirely lacking."[52]

Many biblical scholars consider the apocalyptic literature as a literary genre that was employed to register political protest during a time of social unrest. Himmelfarb cautions, however, that one should not rule out real mystical experiences standing behind the composition of a given apocalypse simply because it has a literary quality or because it lacks instructions for ascent. Although one might suppose that certain of the later hekhalot literature are linked to actual experiences on account of the directions they include for how to achieve such experiences, one should not conclude that an apocalypse is *not* linked to experience just because it fails to provide instructions.[53] Himmelfarb further cautions that, "if visionary experience is reflected in the apocalypses, there are many mirrors between the experience and the text."[54]

Mention has already been made about the fourth Gospel above. It would appear that certain members of the Johannine communities had trained the ability to have mystical experiences wherein they took some

---

51. Lesses, *Ritual Practices*, 16.

52. M. Dean-Otting, *Heavenly Journeys: A Study of the Motif in Hellenistic Jewish Literature* (New York: Verlag Peter Lang, 1984), 263.

53. M. Himmelfarb, "From Prophecy to Apocalypse: The *Book of the Watchers* and Tours of Heaven," in *Jewish Spirituality I: From the Bible through the Middle Ages*, ed. A. Green (New York: Crossroad, 1986), 153.

54. M. Himmelfarb, "Revelation and Rapture: The Transformation of the Visionary in the Ascent Apocalypses," in *Mysteries and Revelations: Studies since the Uppsala Colloquium*, ed. J. J. Collins and J. Charlesworth (Sheffield: Sheffield, 1991), 88.

kind of heavenly journey in order to see the resurrected Lord.[55] The Corinthian believers, too, had had a variety of mystical experiences that provided a profound awareness that the spiritual realm is real. In fact, it was during correspondence with the Corinthians that Paul felt it appropriate to relate that he himself had had an "abundance of revelations." Paul had mystical experiences all the time, he explains, and twice had even traveled (likely) out of his body into paradise to commune with the risen Jesus, presumably viewing members of the heavenly host as well.[56]

I propose, then, that the Scriptures have an internal authority about them that derives precisely from their ability to open up our innermost being to the reality of the heavenly realm and to the singular importance that Jesus Christ plays in mediating that realm to human beings. This is not too different from the approach adapted in the Church of the East. According to the fifth-century Syriac theologian Philoxenus:

> The soul's strength consists in continuous prayer; this clothes the mind in the might which comes from the vision of God. One should read Scripture until the mind has been recollected from wandering thoughts; then, on perceiving in the mind that it has returned to its proper place, having come back to itself from the distraction which is outside it, immediately one should put down the Book and revert to prayer. In this way the reading of Scripture will be for the purpose of prayer, and fasting for the purpose of purity of prayer, and the emptying of thought of all riches will be for the very purpose of prayer. In other words, let the mind do everything requisite in order that it may become worthy to speak with God in prayer.[57]

As C. Rowland explains, Scripture "evokes a perception that pierces beyond the letter. This is the moment of apocalypse when the veil is removed and repentance and epistemological renewal coincide."[58]

That Scripture has the capacity to transform and to awaken the spirit to the heavenly realm is precisely what impels believers to ascribe authority

---

55. Compare J. Kanagaraj, "Jesus the King, Merkabah Mysticism, and the Gospel of John," *Tyndale Bulletin* 47 (1996): 349–66.

56. Compare 2 Kgs 16.17.

57. S. Brock, *The Syriac Fathers on Prayer and the Spiritual Life* (Kalamazoo, MI: Cistercian Publications, 1987), 130.

58. Rowland, "Visionary Experience in Ancient Judaism and Christianity," in *Paradise Now: Essays on Early Jewish and Christian Mysticism*, ed. A. DeConick (Atlanta: Society of Biblical Literature, 2006), 56.

to the Scriptures, authority that is a direct consequence of the way that the Bible is inspired. The Spirit in Scripture and the Spirit in believers "coincides" and arranges for the believers' communion with God. As believers experience this communion, they will have a tendency to react spiritually in much the same way that Nathanael reacted when he met Jesus in John 1: "Rabbi, you are the Son of God! You are the King of Israel!" In other words: "It is in Jesus, the Son of Man, that the real communion with God and communication between heaven and earth is possible, for he is the revelation of God's glory."[59] The Spirit in the Scriptures meets the Spirit in believers, so to speak (after all, it is the same Spirit), allowing us to see what we could not see before: that Jesus is "the mystical way to God."[60] As the Spirit accomplishes this transformation and demonstration of the Scriptures' internal authority, their external authority begins to matter very little, or at least, much less than it did before the mystical experiences began. As the Spirit continues to bring the believer into closer communion with God, both individually and as part of a larger congregation, matters of Biblical inerrancy fade in importance, and one begins to realize that such concerns actually distract the body of Christ from the actual authority that the Bible possesses, an authority that carries even more power. That is, the Bible's authority is steadfastly grounded in its role as a locus around which communion with God is made possible, effected by the Spirit both in the scriptural texts as well as within their readers.

7. Concluding remarks on the role of resurrection-ascension and Scripture's internal authority

Jesus' departure via ascension is presented as a return to glory in the fourth Gospel. By way of her vision, Mary Magdalene becomes the first to understand precisely this: Jesus' ascension is unique in that his ascension to his Father is somehow a *return* to his Father. This revelation has profound implications for those who believe in him. Jesus' death is in some way spiritually intertwined with connecting believers both to Jesus himself (who is now in heaven) and to God (who is also in heaven). M. McNamara points out that the linking of Jesus' death with being taken into heaven was suggested to early Christians by the use of a single Aramaic word that signified

---

59. Kanagaraj, "Jesus the King," 352.
60. Kanagaraj's phrase.

both "to die" and "to be lifted up, exalted."[61] This spiritual insight, delivered to Mary through a vision, is a post-resurrection encounter with Jesus that Dunn states is probably "better described in other than literal terms, since the literalness robs their perceived reality of important dimensions." Through altered states of consciousness, some of the earliest Christians perceived that Christ was somehow not dead even though he had died. Dunn explains, "Luke was attempting to recount something that had 'happened' to Jesus and was of lasting significance for Christians and for the world."[62] This is where the internal authority of Scripture can be seen: that when Christians read it, the Spirit "shows" us both that something extraordinary happened to Jesus and that what happened to him is somehow of lasting importance, not only for believers, but for the entire world.[63]

The Scriptures possess an internal authority, then, by virtue of pointing believers to that reality, the reality that Christ is somehow still alive and that by God's Spirit he is (or can be) alive in us and we in him. This spiritual reality is being made manifest to humans everywhere by way of the Spirit, which is both within humans themselves and also within Scripture. And it is precisely this spiritual connection that inspiration of Scripture affords—the connection between our spirits and the reality of Christ being alive yesterday, today, and forever, as it were—that makes Scripture "internally" authoritative for believers everywhere, both now and on through to the end of the age.

---

61. McNamara, "The Ascension and Exaltation of Christ in the Fourth Gospel," *Scriptura* 19 (1967): 65–73.

62. Dunn, "The Ascension of Jesus: A Test Case for Hermeneutics," in *Auferstehung – Resurrection: The Fourth Durham-Tübingen Research Symposium: Resurrection, Transfiguration and Exaltation in Old Testament, Ancient Judaism and Early Christianity*, ed. F. Avemarie and H. Lichtenberger (Tübingen: Mohr Siebeck, 2001), 319, 321.

63. Compare E. Jones: "I find the most plausible view to be that ascension was purely a spiritual occurrence: the disciples had some sort of experience which assured them of Jesus' triumph over death. . . . In describing the ascension, the first Christian were using contemporary images to convey to others their post-death experience of Jesus." See Jones, "The Origins of 'Ascension' Terminology," *Churchman* 104 (1990): 159, 160.

The Authority of Scripture
Responses

The Authority of Sacred Scriptures

J. Harold Ellens

A SOUND THEOLOGY OF Scripture is the key to authentic faith. This is not only the case for Christian faith but every tradition with a Scripture. Religions are behavioral outgrowths of a person's and community's spirituality. Spirituality has to do with the universal and irrepressible human hunger for meaning. It is an innate drive for profound relationships with others and with God. It is the expression of our inherent desire for eternity, a reaching for the transcendent, a longing for the divine and the eternal.[1]

All religions are grounded in and flow from this spiritual drive. As people grow, develop and think out their worldviews, they acquire meaning, and fashion content that is religious. It becomes natural to look for and create authoritative sources for religion. As a result, traditions of experiences of "meaning-illumination" develop in all religions. Written records describing the original impulse of a given religion—along with subsequent confirmations of the original impulse, as experienced by subsequent believers—form over time and become sacred Scripture.

There is a universal human inclination to nail down tightly the warrants and authority of both the original impulse that lies behind Scripture and the historic development of Scripture through tradition. Humans tend to enshrine both the original impulse and the scriptural witness with sacred status. In Christian tradition, Fundamentalism carries this tendency too far, however, by according authority and "truth-status" to Scripture to the point of idolatrizing it, giving it a virtually magical and mechanical power to dictate comprehensive and unassailable truth for the belief system and moral code of the evangelical and fundamentalist community. This is not

---

1. J. Harold Ellens, *Understanding Religious Experience, What the Bible Says about Spirituality* (Westport: CT: Praeger, 2007).

just true in Christianity. Every religion has its fundamentalist community with its idolatrous approach to sacred Scripture. In my experience, I have interacted with conservative Jews, Muslims, and Hindus, who all fit this unfortunate pattern.

In a system with such a mechanistic theology of Scripture, it becomes necessary for a believer to defend the "truth status" and transcendent authority of every portion of Scripture, lest the failure of one "jot or tittle" to reach that level of authenticity should bring the entire "clockwork orange" crashing down. That is, the evangelical fundamentalist theology of Scripture assumes the utter truth of every element of the historic witness; the authority of the whole depends upon the integrity of every part. Over time, as a result, adherents to that mode of piety have projected upon their Scriptures a sacredness, which derives from their certainty that those historic writings speak with a divine voice. Whether directly written with the finger of God, divinely dictated to the pens of human authors, or generated in their minds and spirits by God's Spirit, the Scriptures are considered to be inspired by God. For fundamentalists, that makes Scripture infallible in its message and inerrant in everything it affirms.

It is well that Carlos Bovell has undertaken to deconstruct that erroneous inerrantist notion and is looking for a way to connect biblical authority to the believers' experience of Christ. The Bible is not a mechanistic object, dropped from heaven, and utterly immune from the vagaries of human cultural influence. An inerrantist theology of Scripture is an idolatrous obscenity that obscures the truth of God and impugns God's reputation. It seriously misrepresents both God's nature and behavior. It is clear from the character and development of the entire created world that God functions in time and space in keeping with the natural laws of development, and by means of the pervasive divine Spirit. That Spirit is the vital force in all living things and the force that keeps the electrons in orbit in the atoms of a rock. It is not that God is incapable of miracles, but rather God prefers to work in the slow and subtle ways of normal life and growth that we see throughout creation.

Moreover, biblical scholars have demonstrated clearly over the last 75–125 years, through careful lexical work in the languages of the ancient Near East, discoveries in archaeology, and a better understanding of ancient historiography, that the Bible is a human book. It contains every type of human literature, such as: songs, essays, proverbs and aphorisms, letters, history, philosophy, theology, and apocalyptic imagination. Much of it is so profound that we must simply acknowledge that it is genuinely inspired and inspiring. In reading some of the Psalms, for example, we are moved by the story of David, an important man with a complicated history: shepherd boy, guerilla fighter, murderer, adulterer, abuser of women, neglecter of his own children, abusive and manipulative king. And yet, even through all this, he was moved by God to write such sublime verses as those found in Psalms 19, 32, 51, 90, 136, 150, and the like.[2]

When trying to incorporate the Bible into psychological counseling, I often find it helpful to group all the literature of the Bible into two basic categories. On the one hand, we have those passages which pronounce clearly God's clean and clear word of radical, unconditional, and universal forgiving grace, for everybody, for everything, for evermore. On the other hand, there is the cultural-historical matrix that *carries* God's clean word of grace, like a rusty old truck carrying an overflowing load of delicious fruit and vegetables to soup kitchens for the needy. In the case of the former, we can easily refer to these passages, since they clearly express God's grace and mercy as "good news," the gospel of God's redeeming grace. In the case of the latter, by contrast, the cultural-historical matrix must be identified as disposable wrappings; *they must be thrown away like garbage*. The two categories of Scripture are radically different. We work against God if we insist on according them equal authority, authenticity, inspiration, or infallibility. It is imperative to understand that the word of God is in the Bible but is not coterminous with the Bible. Not everything between those covers is of equal value, merit, and truth-value.

Indeed, the whole idea of inspiration needs to be revisited. The Bible is a human book, a culturally Jewish book. Both the Old and New Testaments were written by Jews for Jews who, for the most part at least, lived in Jewish communities. Second Temple Judaism cultivated a religio-political outlook that was thoroughly apocalyptic, maintaining that God was caught up in a cosmic war against a spiritual, evil power. The battles were played out both in human history and in the human heart. Our eternal destiny depended upon which side we chose to be on, or upon some arbitrary choice on the part of God before creation. The ultimate outcome for this war was not yet clear in Jesus' time.

Jewish culture inherited some of these ideas from Zoroastrianism during the Babylonian exile. The problem this poses for Scripture is that

2. For a New Testament example, we might look at the letters of Paul.

apocalypticism is completely untrue. More than that, an apocalyptic outlook on life can be psychologically sick and self-destructive to people who adopt it. Was it not apocalyptic fervor that led to the two terrible wars against Rome (67–70 CE and 133–35 CE), resulting in the destruction of Jewish communities in Palestine and Egypt, virtually destroying Judaism? It also got Jesus crucified, leaving an indelible mark on the writings of the New Testament.

By consequence, we must understand that the real word of God is limited to, equivalent to, and coterminous with the passages of universal divine grace, mercy, and forgiveness (such as Gen 12 and 17, Mic 7:18–20, Ps 32, 51, 90, 150, Romans 8, Ephesians 2:8–9, etc). A careful interpretation of Scripture requires knowledge of its languages, history, cultural setting, and relevant archaeological information. Amassing such knowledge is neither an easy nor simple task, but only in this way can we clearly and correctly distinguish between the garbage and the gospel in Scripture and so have a secure foundation for a sound theology of Scripture.

Then we can confidently develop a truly trustworthy and meaningful understanding of God's nature and behavior, and our relationship to God, always standing before God's face.[3] That is the only sure basis for faith, for a belief system, for ethics and a moral code. Everything in faith and theology depends first of all on an authentic theology of Scripture, employed honestly in our personal worldview. It is important to approach the Bible in psychologically healthy ways.

However, an inerrantist will raise an honest objection at this point: "How can you judge that much of the Bible is merely cultural-historical material and not the word of God, and then have any basis to claim that any part of the Bible is inspired by God's spirit and has divine authority?" That is a fair question. The answer, however, is not nearly as difficult as most people make it out to be. It amounts simply to this: *Take your stand at the foot of the cross*. Let yourself be soaked through thoroughly with what we can see about the nature and behavior of God from the perspective at the foot of the cross. There, we cannot fail to miss the amazing extent to which God will go to demonstrate for us, and get across to us, the length, and breadth, and depth of his love and grace to us.

Once you are imbued with that sense of reality, you can look back down the corridors of Old Testament times and ask what rings true to the

---

3. J. Harold Ellens, *Honest Faith for our Time, Truth-telling about the Bible, the Creed, and the Church* (Eugene, OR: Pickwick, 2010).

vision as seen from the foot of the cross. In the same way, you can look forward through the cadences of the New Testament story and ask what rings true to the vision as seen from the foot of the cross. In both cases, it becomes immediately clear that only grace, mercy, and forgiveness ring true because this is what we experience at the foot of the cross. By contrast, the extermination of the Canaanites does not ring true; the casting of countless sinners into hellfire does not ring true. John's claim that God so loves the world that he came to save it—not judge and condemn it (Jn 3:16–17)—*does* ring true, and so on.

So that which rings true to the gospel of grace is the clean word of God. That which does not so ring true is not the authoritative word of God, the God of grace, mercy, and peace.

Even if my inerrantist inquisitor were to agree with all this, he might ask another question, in order to be honest to his inquiry: "In what sense, then, can you say that the Bible or parts of it are inspired?" That, too, is a fair and decent question; it must be asked and answered. The most satisfactory answer is one that has been around since the Reformation of the church in the 16th and 17th centuries.[4] It is best epitomized in a remark made by the biblical scholar, Marcus Borg, nearly a decade ago.[5] He said that Jesus was divine revelation to us in that he was a man whose life was full of God. I extrapolate from that that the authors of Scripture who authentically

---

4. The Protestant Reformers, Luther, Calvin, Zwingli, and the others called their notion of inspiration, "organic inspiration of Scripture." That has been the official position on inspiration in the Reformation traditions of Lutheran, Reformed, United Church of Christ, and Presbyterian Churches ever since. The position holds that the individual words and sentences, or even chapters or books in Scripture, were not what was inspired. Inspiration of Scripture meant that the very organism of the author's person was so filled with the presence of God that the author of Scripture could express so authentically his or her vision of the nature of God, and the way in which God was operating, that the picture he or she painted, so to speak, gave us God's truth. They recognized that some of the authors of Scripture envisioned the picture accurately and others did not. Luther said that the Epistle of James was an epistle of straw and should be thrown out of the Bible; and the Book of Revelation was such a mess, theologically and historically, that it should never have been included in the Bible in the first place. It is said that, when the bishops at the Counsel of Nicaea voted on what should be included in the Bible, the Book of Revelation made it by only a one vote margin, hardly a robust endorsement. The mechanistic and magical notion of inspiration conjured up by Evangelical Fundamentalism did not come into use until the 19th century, and only in America. It is a relatively recent American heresy. Unfortunately, many inerrantists are under the false notion that it goes back to Jesus. This is simply not the case.

5. In a lecture at the First Presbyterian Church of Ann Arbor, Michigan, 2008.

expressed the divine words of God's grace were the ones who spoke or wrote from a life that was full of God.

It seems very clear that all the authors whose work was incorporated into the Old and New Testaments believed they were telling the real story about the mighty acts of God in the history of Israel.[6] Most were persons who lived their lives in profound awareness of personal communion with God; they could feel their lives filled with divine presence. Out of that sense of living in communion with God they committed to writing their understanding of life, interpreting history as the stage for the mighty acts of God. Sometimes, they got it right, but other times their stories were just conveying erroneous opinions regarding what was actually unfolding.

When the Israelites confused an egregious foreign policy with the will and mandate of God, they got it wrong. When, on the other hand, Abraham (Gen 12 and 17), David (Ps 32 and 52), and Micah (7:18–20) perceived the radical nature of God's universal grace, they got it right. In the same manner, when Paul (Rom 8; Eph 2) and John (3:16–17, 5:27–47, and throughout the fourth gospel) declared God's intent to save every human being in the end, they got it right.

Hence, Paul could enunciate in all of his epistles that on the last day, "every eye shall see God, every knee shall bow to God, and every tongue shall confess that Christ is Lord, to the glory of God the Father." Paul knew that Jesus intended exactly that. He confidently and sincerely declared the word of God, understanding, by the testimony of the prophets and apostles, and by the divine Spirit with which his life was filled, the clear word of grace that God was revealing all throughout the history of God's people.

That raises, of course, a final question that my inerrantist colleague will be compelled to ask me out of sheer honesty: "By what *authority* can I arbitrarily claim that it is the biblical word of radical divine grace for every human that is the clear word of God, and that none other is?" That is, perhaps, the best question of all, and its answer is also the most gratifying.

I am a biblical theologian by training and a psychologist by profession. Therefore, I am deeply interested in both the theological interpretation and the psychological interpretation of Scripture. When it comes down to it, what we want to understand about the Bible is what it has to say about the nature and function of God, what it has to say about the nature and function of human beings, and, most of all, how both of these relate to our

---

6. See Frank Moore Cross, *Magnalia Dei, The Mighty Acts of God, in Memoriam of G. Ernest Wright* (New York: Doubleday, 1976).

spiritual life and growth. My approach to the psychological interpretation of biblical texts has always been primarily from the operational or applied side. Then, I move on to considering conceptual, theoretical and theological models. In both content and method, I always strive to maintain a dual emphasis on theology and psychology. I think Bovell is right to insist that Scripture's inspiration and authority is ultimately connected to how it is applied and interpreted by believers.

Personally, I try to operate, like Isaac Newton, with three basic laws of biblical interpretation:

1. *It is necessary to separate the garbage from the gospel in the Bible in order to discern what the word of God is when reading biblical narratives.* The garbage is the cultural-historical matrix in which the essential message is conveyed. The gospel is the clear word of grace which is conveyed, wherever it breaks out and can be discerned clearly and cogently in the biblical text.

2. *That which, in the Bible, is psychospiritually destructive for any person is not the divine word. That which is psychospiritually constructive for persons is the divine word of God.* That word will always be a word about grace.

3. *Use of the psychological lens is essential for determining what in the biblical narratives is psychospiritually constructive or destructive for human beings.* The warrant for divine truth in anything is that it is psychospiritually healing for people. Whether a word is *psychologically* sound and constructive or healing is the criterion for divine truth.

Further explanation

1. That the word of God is always the word of grace is not arguable. It is simply the claim I make, and its warrant is that *only it* heals and enhances a person's spirituality.

2. In my model, God is, by definition, a God of thoroughly unconditional, radical, and universal grace. Any God that is not a God of such grace, is, by definition, not God, but is a monster. Any idea any human conjures up about God as not, by definition, a God of grace is corrupt,

monstrous, and confused, because it demonstrably damages rather than heals.

3. God is subtle and not obvious in the world and in human experience. So we must take a psychological lens and look at the subtle intimations of God's presence and nature in history, life, and our personal experience. These subtle intimations include a) the mindfulness of creation, b) the benevolence of providence, c) the natural urge in all things toward beauty, d) the fact that unconditional acceptance and forgiveness is the only ultimate healing force in life, and e) the fact that this kind of service of grace is precisely tailored to our central need for healing that sets us free for spiritual growth, the healing of forgiveness, and the joy of life lived for God in spite of our human flaws, sins, and iniquity.

4. The warrant for what is real and true is what *works*. Only the equation of grace works in the ultimate healing, growth, maturation, and wholeness for which human beings have the potential and are, therefore, inherently destined.

5. Therefore, we must conclude that, by definition, God is a God of grace. The fact that only this definition of God works for our healing, growth, maturation, and wholeness confirms that it is the only rational and psychospiritually authentic way to conceptualize God. All other conceptualizations are deficient, destructive, and hence, monstrous.

This perspective on Scripture—focusing only on biblical content that is sacred, holy, and true—affords the Bible, and God's word in it, much deeper reverence and more profound esteem for the truth of God than the mechanistic model of evangelical inerrancy. Moreover, it allows God to stand up more majestically and warmheartedly toward us than there is ever room for God to be in the rigid legalisms that tend to characterize Evangelicalism and Fundamentalism.

A "Reflexive Trust" in the Authority of Scripture

Holly Beers

THE WORLD IS INDEED a strange place. As I was reading Bovell's two chapters on the external and internal authority of Scripture, I reflected on my own background and academic journey. I hail from a Midwestern slice of evangelical Pentecostalism. Those two labels are not a contradiction in terms, or in my church, at least, they were not. We insisted *both* that we had a high view of Scripture (and accordingly tossed around words such as "inerrant" and "infallible") *and* that the Spirit speaks continually, personally, and often surprisingly through the text to us today. Whether or not the Spirit's speaking coincided with an official "inerrantist" reading was not a concern, as inerrancy for us did not include a strong historical-critical frame for reading the text. This created a space of comfort, for we were able to insist that the Bible was an error-free zone without having to be confronted with any "errors" (as the historical-critical frame is likely to point out). We knew, we *lived*, the Bible's surprising openness, mediated through the power of the Spirit of God. What that environment created in me was a "reflexive trust" in Scripture (as my Westmont colleague Telford Work recently named it), a trust that could handle ambiguity and epistemological uncertainty, though I did not have the language for it during my childhood and adolescence. My academic journey would lead me to those epistemological spaces, however, and now here we are. In light of this quick autobiographical tour, I have three main areas of comment: one commendation, one commendation plus question(s), and one question.

I applaud Bovell's frames of "external" and "internal" authority. He follows Bauckham's notion of external authority as "where a person accepts a statement, command or prescription because the person making it is qualified to make it," and then proposes: "the core of the New Testament's 'external' authority is grounded in the fact that the earliest NT books contain traditions and teachings that grew out of the experience of believers who saw God when the risen Jesus appeared to them by the power of the Holy Spirit" (59). As Bovell's intended audience would claim an evangelical identity, his explication is helpful and probably meant to reassure; it is common coin in evangelical circles to stress both "earliness" and the experiences of the early believers. The same is true for the way in which Bovell frames his notion of "internal" authority (also following Bauckham), which, again, I appreciate: "internal" authority is "a case where a statement made, command issued, or prescription offered convinces a person on its own merits" (59). Bovell wants to link "Scripture's authority to Jesus continuing activity in 'appearing' to believers today," adding that "upon reading Scripture (or hearing Scripture being read), believers find that the Christian Bible is a provision from God to Spirit-filled Christians, which acts as a means of grace for communing with him" (91). Again, the claim that believers experience God through Scripture feels "typically" evangelical, as does his clarification that this communion with the divine has a Christocentric focus. To my mind, what will be more surprising is the claim that, through Scripture, Jesus mediates the heavenly "realm to human beings" (108). Of course, if Jesus is in heaven and believers experience Jesus through the text, Jesus is thus mediating the heavenly realm. The key piece seems to be the means of verification: it is through believers' *experience*.

This focus on experience leads to my second reflection, which I both appreciate and question in terms of the extent to which he takes it. Bovell correctly insists that "it is the hermeneutical role of the Bible's believing readers that at least partly confers authority on Scripture" (59). The reality that readers (in, dare we say, their subjectivity?!) are part of the process of performing the Bible's authority becomes clear when it is realized that one cannot objectively prove it. Evangelical readers of the Bible are part of a community of people who have given allegiance to a larger narrative or frame that includes the prominence of these texts (as opposed to other texts) for shaping belief and action.

So far so good. Where Bovell travels next, however, raises a few critical questions for me. He mentions the reality of what he calls "pluralism," stressing how common it is within Protestantism and asking if it should be considered to be problematic. He states: "To wit, interpretive pluralism is precisely what one will *expect* because the very process of inspiring the Bible is intrinsically tied to the spiritual, hermeneutical activity of the interpreters themselves. This means that the inspiration of the Bible is a dynamic, ongoing process that is never discursively finished" (62). Though I could quibble with the language (for example, choosing the arguably more inflammatory word "pluralism" rather than something like "diversity"), my bigger question concerns unity. Within this "pluralism," as Bovell sees it, is there still unity? If I am reading him correctly, he seems to see the Christological focus as a unifying factor, for this is true even of allegorical interpretation.

Indeed, he appears to give high marks to allegorical interpretation both ancient and modern (which is reminiscent of some strands of the current "biblical theology" movement), stressing the high view of Scripture to which allegorical interpreters often adhere. His defense of allegory carries with it the irony (to my mind) that the official protest against allegorical interpretation in many evangelical circles conflicts with the reality of common allegorical practices, especially in relation to narrative texts. The focus on history, and "proving" that the events in biblical narrative texts actually happened, can easily lead to an allegorical *application* to/for today's church. An example might be the David and Goliath story in 1 Samuel 17, where, after sorting through the issue of when David first met Saul and proving that it is possible for Goliath to be as tall as the text claims, the application functions allegorically in that modern-day believers are now "David" and must conquer the "Goliath" of sin, addiction, a human enemy, etc., in their lives. So here I am sympathetic to Bovell's arguments that the evangelical focus on history has overplayed its hand. However, I am not sure that de-historicizing narrative texts that are apparently intended to have at least some historical grounding solves the problem (especially because it creates another one). I would suggest that a better next step is to pay closer attention, and teach evangelicals in general to pay closer attention, to the various genres in the Bible. Narrative communicates truth differently than letters and/or the various poetic forms, and a robust view of the Bible's authority must be able to incorporate the Bible's diversity (or should I say plurality?) in this area.

Back to allegory: I realize that it is considered inappropriate in some circles to critique the church fathers and their use of allegory, and I do not want to fall prey to what C.S. Lewis famously called chronological snobbery.[1] However, to approve without reserve seems to ignore the very

---

1. C.S. Lewis. *Surprised by Joy* (Harcourt, 1955), 207, discusses his friend Barfield and comments: "In the first place he made short work of what I have called my 'chronological

important point that, based on the evidence we have, many church fathers were not very well attuned to the Jewishness of the texts that we call the New Testament (and the Old Testament, for that matter). That they read the Scripture from within their own contexts and lenses goes without saying, for all humans read Scripture in that way. However, to give up or downplay the pursuit of the Jewish context feels not only inconsistent with Bovell's practice elsewhere of utilizing the Second Temple Jewish context/world, but leans toward an epistemological copout. It is not enough to talk about the "endless rewriting of texts in a chain of commentary that can never be arrested" (69). While that may be the historical reality, we have more options than equal approval of every commentary in the chain. It is possible to argue that there are appropriate parameters in the interpretation of the New Testament texts without also arguing that we have perfect access to and embodiment of those parameters (and thus interpretive perfection). Also, while I am sensitive to issues of power and oppression in interpretation, appropriate respect for the *other* (whoever it may be) is seemingly better demonstrated in engagement (even if that engagement takes the shape of critical disagreement) than the avoidance that a blanket approval allows.[2]

In reference to the Old Testament, Bovell stresses that, for Christians, its authority was different prior to the resurrection. I agree, and am sympathetic to his insistence that a post-resurrection reading of the Old Testament yielded new light. Jesus is the hermeneutical lens through which his followers read their Scriptures. Because of this, I also agree with Bovell that a "predictive" pointing to Jesus is not clear in the Old Testament and has thus been inappropriately used in some evangelical circles. However, I would suggest that a better understanding of the hermeneutics of the New Testament writers can be achieved through immersion in the Second Temple Jewish world, not that of the (non-Jewish) church fathers.[3] To group

---

snobbery,' the uncritical acceptance of the intellectual climate common to our own age and the assumption that whatever has gone out of date is on that account discredited." To my mind, chronological snobbery evinces a "modern," Enlightenment notion of progress.

2. For a more nuanced discussion, see chapter 2, "Intertextuality—Philosophy and Method," in Beers, *The Followers of Jesus as the "Servant": Luke's Model from Isaiah for the Disciples in Luke-Acts* (New York: T&T Clark, 2015), 6–30.

3. I would argue this even while granting at least some credence to Bovell's claim that "by putting *the specific question of Jesus* to the OT, [the disciples were] thereby introducing a radically new hermeneutical impetus to their Second Temple exegetical approaches to Scripture" (83).

the church fathers' hermeneutical practice generically with that of the New Testament writers appears a bit imprecise and thus unhelpful.[4]

Also in relationship to the Old Testament, Second Temple Judaism demonstrates the common use of and authority given to the LXX, a trait shared with the New Testament writers. Because of this, I resonate with Bovell's argument that "different believing communities are free to develop and adopt different OT canons as they see fit for the purposes of understanding Christ as the culmination of God's revelation to humankind" (86). In a footnote on the same page he mentions the Roman Catholic and Eastern churches, lest any good evangelical see him (too quickly) including heretical sects or cults.

Now to my third point. Perhaps my biggest question concerns Bovell's comments on the resurrection. For Bovell, the resurrection appearances are what he calls "mystical experiences" and/or "altered states of consciousness." Perhaps my critique lies partly with the quasi-psychological language,[5] though the bigger question concerns the nature of the resurrection appearances themselves. If I am reading Bovell correctly, he seems willing to admit that the disciples' "mystical experiences" and "altered states of consciousness" were real experiences, though Jesus in a "real" resurrection body was not. He quotes O'Collins with approval: "the resurrection is not an event *in* space and time and hence should not be called historical [since t]hrough the resurrection Christ . . . moves outside the world and its history, outside the ordinary datable, localizable conditions of our experience—to become an 'otherwordly' reality" (94).

I am happy to admit that the resurrection does not fit neatly into human conceptions of space and time, though I would want to frame this epistemologically. In terms of what humans can know and explain in our "space and time," are we not limited by our language? In other words, can we say that it is impossible to describe post-resurrection reality with pre-resurrection language? But can that "post-resurrection reality" still be real? When confronted with a Jesus who gives permission to touch him (Luke

---

4. At least twice during the last several years of ETS and/or SBL annual meetings, I have heard Rikki Watts make similar comments during sessions. Also, in my own research on the use of the Isaianic servant passages, I found the interpretive approach(es) in Second Temple Jewish circles to be quite different from that of the church fathers, the latter of whom tended to read Jesus directly into the Isaianic passages (without a great degree of nuancing).

5. I thank my friend and mentor Dr. Thorsten Moritz for this insight, shared in conversation on January 28, 2015.

24:39; John 20:27), and who eats (Luke 24:42–43), but also is unrecognizable at times and can walk through walls (Luke 24:16; John 20:26), how might the disciples explain it? They cannot describe it fully, completely, "historically." They can only compare it to what they know, this side of the resurrection. Moritz calls such language "analogical; it is 'as-if' language."[6]

In other words, while I am sensitive to Bovell's critique of the overfocus by some evangelicals on history, and agree that John 20 may not be "aiming to provide a straightforward, publicly accessible account of what 'really' happened," does that mean that we are now in the realm of "altered states of consciousness?" Or could this "altered state of consciousness" be the human accessing of the very real realm of heaven? Heaven is the appropriate realm for resurrection bodies, it would seem. Are these resurrection appearances then tastes of the overlap or merging of heaven and earth, after which the disciples are left to their "earthly" language to explain? With this nuance I would agree with Bovell's claim that "the fact that Jesus was 'raised from the dead' is not something that a person would have concluded by their own powers of deduction. A special dispensation of the Spirit is required for the realization that a 'resurrection' took place" (100). It does seem likely that only Jesus' followers are granted access to the merging of heaven and earth in the resurrection appearances. Or perhaps we agree more than I realize, as Bovell's comments in a footnote regarding Christ "being alive in some 'alternate' reality" and his description of John 20:11–16 as "a mythical, narrative 'space' where heaven and earth so conspicuously overlap" may suggest?

In light of this, I find dissatisfying Bovell's suggestion "we ought not conceive of Christ's resurrection as the basis for a future resurrection of humans. In my own view, it is much more fruitful to think of an ongoing resurrection of humans that is already taking place—*that Christ participated in and transformed by participating in it*—which serves as the basis for Christ's resurrection" (94). While I also see the NT stressing the "already" or "ongoing" piece and the empowerment that it brings to the daily lives of believers, I hesitate to place all the stress on such a realized eschatology. The "not yet" piece is emphasized by Paul in passages that include 1 Corinthians 15:1–58, 2 Corinthians 5:1–10, and Romans 8:18–25. That Paul ties Jesus' bodily resurrection to the future bodily resurrection of believers (e.g. 1 Cor.

---

6. Though the specific language was given in conversation with my mentor Dr. Thorsten Moritz on January 28, 2015, the roots of this discussion began in 2003 and have continued since then.

15:20–23), and then uses analogical language (i.e. pre-resurrection language) to describe the post-resurrection body (1 Cor. 15:35–49) makes me hesitant to downplay or ignore the "realness" of future, not-yet, resurrection bodies for believers. Also, since I often see members of the evangelical world submitting to a fairly spiritualized version of the Christian faith, I would suggest that many in that world need a better (Jewish/New Testament) grounding in the goodness of the physical world, our bodies included.[7]

In short, it seems to me that a humble awareness of our epistemological condition, or the partiality of our knowledge (and language), addresses both the problem that Bovell sees and critiques his critique of it. While we cannot (and should not) claim objectivity in our historical knowledge of the Bible (as a/the foundation for the Bible's authority), I do not see our best option as lauding an interpretive openness even for varied allegorical readings. Might we speak of a "reflexive trust" in Scripture, grounded *not only* in the earliness of our texts (and their roots in the experiences of early believers) and the appearance of Jesus to believers today in and through those texts? Might we be able to add a balanced focus on history and genre, framed within an epistemology that acknowledges partial knowledge while at the same time groans with the Spirit for what we will someday fully know (in the fullest sense)? Perhaps this is my pentecostal intuition speaking. But then again, perhaps Scripture itself encourages us in our already and not-yet reality, and with Paul, we can say: "and not only the creation, but we ourselves, who have the first fruits of the Spirit, groan inwardly while we wait for adoption, the redemption of our bodies. For in hope we were saved. Now hope that is seen is not hope. For who hopes for what is seen? But if we hope for what we do not see, we wait for it with patience" (Rom. 8:23–25).

---

7. Bovell also cites 1 John 3:2: "we are God's children now; what we will be has not yet been revealed. What we do know is this: when he is revealed, we will be like him, for we will see him as he is." However, in light of 1 John's emphasis on Jesus' physicality (e.g. 1:1; 4:2), probably because of some gnostic tendencies, the "as he is" language appears to point to a "physical" body of some kind.

Jesus' Post-Resurrection Appearances in the Light of Full-Bodied Spirit Materializations

Clint Tibbs

CARLOS BOVELL DEALS WITH why he believes the Bible *should* be authoritative. He does not appeal to the usual cases for authority of Scripture, e.g. Scripture is the word of God, and the canon of Scripture. Instead, Bovell appeals to 1) a Christocentric principle, namely Jesus' post-resurrection appearances, for describing the external authority of the Bible and 2) a pneumatological principle, namely a personal reading of Scripture guided by the Spirit, for describing the internal authority of the Bible. Whereas the latter has a history going back as far as Augustine (divine illumination), the former, and quite early on, was thought to be a settled case: the resurrection appearances of Jesus were that of his physical, flesh, blood, and bone body. Bovell's Christocentric principle not only appears in his argument for an external authority of Scripture but also in his argument for an internal authority of Scripture. For this reason, I would like to focus on Jesus' post-resurrection appearances because Bovell places a high priority on them for Scripture's authority.

Bovell is keenly aware of the historical difficulty posed by the Old Testament in claiming that Jesus' resurrection gives authority to *all* Christian Scriptures that include the Old Testament. Bovell, like an erudite historian, places himself in the shoes of first-century Jewish readers and imagines what kind of difficulty the Old Testament posed for the Jesus movement. The difficulty is this: How (and when) was *this* Jesus found in the Old Testament? How could reading Jesus back into the Old Testament (Septuagint) be a legitimate interpretation of Jewish Scripture? Did the Apostles and

Jesus' Post-Resurrection Appearances

their followers ever read the Old Testament as a narrative about Jesus? After all, very early on Paul actually identifies the "rock" that accompanied Moses and the Hebrews in the desert as Christ Himself (1 Cor 10:4); Paul puts Jesus into the Old Testament Scriptures.

Bovell is not arguing whether reading Jesus back into the Old Testament actually happened (because it did happen) but rather Bovell is interested in how such a thing *could* have happened. Answering this question helps explain Bovell's thesis for why the Scriptures are authoritative. He proposes that the authority of Scripture for followers of Jesus was established on one particular event: Jesus' resurrection, particularly the post-resurrection *appearances* of Jesus to various individuals and how these appearances provided the evidence that *this* Jesus is found in the Old Testament Scriptures. Bovell wants to ground the authority of the Scriptures in what he calls the mystical experiences and the altered states of consciousness of individuals who experienced Jesus after his resurrection. These experiences are linked directly to divine activity; hence the intervention of God in the lives of the Apostles and early Christians is the important thing here for authority. The early Christian Scriptures are a record of God's dealings with those who came to recognize *this* Jesus as the Messiah *because* of his resurrection.

I am sympathetic to Bovell's focus on the mystical (I prefer "spirit") experiences of the early Christians as a means to understand their worldview. After all, the New Testament is full of episodes in the lives of the Apostles and others that deal with what is commonly known today as "supernatural" experiences: experiences of the risen Jesus, of the appearance of angels, out-of-body experiences, exorcism, speaking "in a spirit," and heavenly journeys. These experiences pose a problem for the modern exegete who has no personal experience of these types from which to draw in order to come to grips with some of the transcendental episodes recorded in the New Testament, e.g. Jesus' transfiguration and Paul's out-of-body experience. The lack of transcendental experience provides a ready-made scenario that easily dismisses such episodes as literary fictions or something exegetically glossed over as a figment of a "pre-critical" era in human history.

When an Apostle sees the risen Jesus, what *exactly* does he see? The Apostles were familiar with resuscitations as in the case of Jairus' daughter (Luke 8:54–55) and Lazarus (John 11:43–44). But in Jesus' case physical demise meant the end of his earthly life as a human being ("He gave up the ghost" was a euphemism for physical death). He was not physically resuscitated, for his post-resurrection appearances were *resurrection* appearances which, according to Paul, do not include flesh and blood (1 Cor 15:50). Yet Luke records a very physical resurrection appearance: "See my hands and my feet, that it is I myself; touch me and see, for a spirit does not have flesh and bones as you see that I have" (Luke 24:39). What is going on here?

Bovell compares Jesus' post-resurrection appearances to "heavenly journeys" and "visions" in apocalyptic literature of the period. Since Bovell's thesis for Scriptures' authority is premised on the appearances of Jesus after his death, I would like to provide another source apart from Jewish apocalyptic literature for explaining some of these phenomena, thereby strengthening and elaborating Bovell's thesis for Scripture's authority. The seeming contradiction between Paul's apparent non-physical resurrection and Luke's physical resurrection is actually no contradiction at all if we resort to the phenomenon known as spirit materialization in the case of Luke's physical descriptions of Jesus' post-resurrection appearances.

I hope that Bovell's readers do not find my use of data on spirit materializations as heterodox. After all, Bovell's talk about "mystical experiences" and "altered states of consciousness" advances the discussion into an area that is covered by terms such as "paranormal phenomena" and "psychical phenomena," terms often employed when discussing the manifestation of spirits (possession, materializations, etc.), psychic phenomena such as ESP, out-of-body experiences, and mediumship. There are clear enough analogues between spirit phenomena as recorded in Scripture (and the ancient world) and spirit phenomena occurring today (studied by anthropologists, sociologists, psychologists, historians, theologians, philosophers, and scientists) to warrant the use of modern research into spirit phenomena as a means to understand the scriptural accounts.[1] Scripture usually does not explain how spirit phenomena occur or even when a spirit phenomenon *is*

---

1. Research grossly mislabeled as "psychical research"—for this term suggests that *all* of the phenomena originate in the *psyche*, i.e. the mind, of an individual. Studies on modern investigations into spirit phenomena include the following: John J. Cerullo, *The Secularization of the Soul: Psychical Research in Modern Britain* (Philadelphia: Institute for the Study of Human Issues, 1982); Janet Oppenheim, *The Other World: Spiritualism and Psychical Research in England, 1850–1914* (New York: Cambridge University Press, 1985); John Warne Monroe, *Laboratories of Faith: Mesmerism, Spiritism, and Occultism in Modern France* (Ithaca, NY: Cornell University Press, 2008); Heather Wolffram, *The Stepchildren of Science: Psychical Research and Parapsychology in Germany, c. 1870–1939* (New York: Rodopi, 2009); M. Brady Brower, *Unruly Spirits: The Science of Psychic Phenomena in Modern France* (Urbana, IL: University of Illinois Press, 2010); and Sofie Lachapelle, *Investigating the Supernatural: From Spiritism and Occultism to Psychical Research and Metaphysics in France, 1853–1931* (Baltimore, MD: Johns Hopkins University Press, 2011).

occurring.² The New Testament scholar, Dale C. Allison, remarks about the use of research into modern spirit phenomena as a way to understand biblical reports: "Psychical researchers, just like Christian apologists, have long used precisely the same two reported facts—collective appearances and multiple recipients—to argue that certain reported apparitions are somehow veridical."³

A prejudice, however, still exists among scholars who regard claims to paranormal phenomena as products of cultures deemed unscientific and uncritical according to western standards, i.e., non-western cultures that have not experienced the benefits of philosophy, western medicine, the Scientific Revolution, or the Enlightenment. This prejudice leads to the conclusion: belief or claims in paranormal phenomena are superstitions that can be explained as inexplicable natural phenomena or organic aberrations (e.g. hallucinations) rather than spirits and demons.

Both scientists and theologians shun paranormal phenomena but for different reasons.⁴ This shun originates partly in early modern physics (sev-

---

2. How many readers think, "Aha! Spirit phenomenon!" when reading the physical descriptions of Jesus' post-resurrection appearances in Luke and John? Hardly a one. Some even insist against it. Joel B. Green remarks, "Jesus grounds the continuity of his identity ('It is really me!'), first, in his materiality, his physicality—in the constitution of flesh and density of bones: 'Look at my hands and my feet; see that it is I myself. Touch me and see; for a ghost does not have flesh and bones as you see that I have' (24:39). Here is no phantom, no vision, no spirit-being" ("Resurrection of the Body: New Testament Voices Concerning Personal Continuity and the Afterlife," in *What About the Soul: Neuroscience and Christian Anthropology* [Nashville, TN: Abingdon, 2004], 85–99, here 92).

3. Dale C. Allison, *Resurrecting Jesus: The Earliest Christian Tradition and its Interpreters* (New York: T & T Clark, 2005), 270. Other scholars who have used paranormal research to inform classical and biblical reports of spirit phenomena are Eric R. Dodds, *The Greeks and the Irrational* (Berkeley: University of California, 1951); Robert R. Wilson, *Prophecy and Society in Ancient Israel* (Philadelphia: Fortress, 1980); and Craig S. Keener, "Spirit Possession as a Cross-Cultural Experience," *BBR* 20.2 (2010): 215–36. See further Jacob Bazak, *Judaism and Psychical Phenomena: A Study of Extrasensory Perception in Biblical, Talmudic, and Rabbinical Literature in the Light of Contemporary Parapsychological Research* (New York: Garrett, 1972); Evelyn Garth Moore, *Try the Spirits: Christianity and Psychical Research* (New York: Oxford University Press, 1977); John J. Heaney, *The Sacred and the Psychic: Parapsychology and Christian Theology* (Ramsey, NJ: Paulist, 1984); and Brian Inglis, *Natural and Supernatural: A History of the Paranormal from the Earliest Times to 1914* (London: White Crow, 2012).

4. See Carl B. Becker (*Paranormal Experience and Survival of Death* [Albany, NY: State University of New York Press, 1993]) who states, "Paranormal phenomena ranging from spirit possession and astral travel to resuscitation of the dead have been known for thousands of years in Europe as well as Asia. They have been consistently banned and suppressed by the church, not because their reality was doubted but because they were

enteenth century) during which time the western worldview was divided into two substances: the physical and the non-physical. The ancient worldview, however, was not so demarcated. Even though we find a kind of matter-spirit dualism implicit in ancient Greek philosophers, namely Parmenides (who distinguished between the reasoning faculty and the physical senses), Plato (who distinguished between the intelligible world of Forms and the sensible world of physical objects and images), and Neoplatonism, it is not until the seventeenth century, primarily in the work of René Descartes, that a single term came to be employed as a cover for all objects to which the science of physical motion applied; that term was "matter."[5]

In Descartes we find, for the first time, a clear demarcation between two substances: body (*res extensa*) and soul (*res cogitans*). The former is an extended thing, which is made up of matter, and exists insofar as there is space for it to exist. The latter is an unextended thing, and therefore is not composed of a body, because only bodies can extend into space. Critics of Descartes argued that an unextended thing cannot exist if it does not extend into a space. Otherwise, *where* is it?[6] Thus, the science of physics was

---

dangerous, opening the gates to heterodoxy and perhaps to the work of the devil himself. Scientists, too, have very human religious commitments and presuppositions. In some cases these involve rejecting survival as impossible or unimportant, in others, of limiting it to articles of faith, consciously segregated from the sorts of issues held to be open to scientific inquiry. The evidence that persons are more than material or that life might survive the grave is a mind-boggling proposition to many dogmatic people who quickly anathematize it" (143).

5. Originally in Greek *hulē* meant "woodland," "brushwood," and "timbre." As a technical term for "matter" in the sense of "*the stuff* of which a thing is made," i.e., "material," *hulē* was employed as such initially by Aristotle. See *Metaphysics* 1032a17, "Natural generation is the generation of things whose generation is by nature. That from which they are generated is what we call matter (*hulēn*)." See H. G. Liddell and R. Scott, *Greek-English Lexicon* (Oxford: Clarendon, 1996), *s.v.* "hulē."

6. The modern-day common conception for a soul as an incorporeal, immaterial yet conscious entity, a "disembodied soul," originates in Descartes' *Meditations*. But the Cartesian soul does not adequately reflect the ancient worldview of spirits or souls. For one thing, the term soul (*psuchē*) was multifaceted in the ancient world. It might mean "vital power" that enlivens the human body or it might be used to refer to a conscious bodily entity that survives the death of the human body. See Dwight J. Ingle, "Psyche in Ancient Greek Thought," *Perspectives in Biology and Medicine* 31 (1988): 264–84. We cannot call forth Cartesian dualism as an early-modern example for an ancient spirit-independent-of-matter dualism, for the simple reason that Descartes' soul, or *res cogitans*, although independent of the body, did not extend into space, unlike the ancient worldview of souls and spirits that had bodies extending into space (Plato, however, is inconsistent). Descartes' soul is better understood as a metaphysicalized Aristotelian soul, i.e. a soul that functions at the biological level (so Aristotle; note Descartes' pineal gland

a science of matter, a science whereby the category for soul (and all things pertaining to other-worldly "spirit") was entirely removed from the interests of physics because such a category, in Cartesian terms, did not require a space in which something to extend. This space was, of course, the crucible in which physics did its work.[7] Descartes had created the very categories that westerners today unwittingly use to talk about this world (the world physicists study) and the next world (the world of heaven and spirits).[8]

Descartes' two categories, however, do not so easily fit first-century thought. Whereas one can, indeed, discern a matter/body—spirit/mind dualism in ancient thought, the line drawn between the two was not so sharp and distinct at that time. The worldview of the ancients was marked by a constellation of terms for human bodies and its parts such as *sōma*, *skēnē*, *ostea*, *haima*, and *sarx*, for spirit bodies such as *pneuma*, *daimonion*, and *psuche*, as well as for "fine" (less dense) material bodies that ambiguously fell between the physical reality and spirit reality of the ancients: *aēr*, *thumos*, and *puros*.[9] Even the more abstract notions of incorporeality (*asōmatos*) and immateriality (*ahulos*) originate in Greek thinking, particularly in Plato (*asōmatos*) and Aristotle (*asōmatos* and *ahulos*).[10] Jesus'

---

connection) yet is not dependent on the body for its survival after the body's demise. Aristotle, however, does refer to a *nous* that enters the body from without and survives its death. See Renehan, "Greek Origins," 136, n. 70. Also, Aristotle's God, the Unmoved Mover, does not extend into space and is incorporeal just like Descartes' *res cogitans*. Thomas Hobbes would call both Aristotle and Descartes to task on unextendedness and incorporeality as categories for angels and God. For Hobbes, nothing can be unless it fills a space, and only bodies can fill a space. Hobbes was no innovator in this respect, for the fourth-century Church Fathers claimed that God and the angels had bodies made of substance. See Samuel I. Mintz, *The Hunting of Leviathan* (New York: Cambridge University Press, 1962), 88–90; and Gary B. Herbert, "Hobbes's Phenomenology of Space," *Journal of the History of Ideas* 48 (1987): 709–17.

7. See Richard S. Westfall, *The Construction of Modern Science: Mechanisms and Mechanics* (New York: Cambridge University Press, 1997), "The effect of Cartesian dualism ... was to excise every trace of the psychic from material nature with surgical precision, leaving it a lifeless field knowing only the brute blows of inert chunks of matter. ... Virtually every scientist of importance in the second half of the century accepted as beyond question the dualism of body and soul. The physical nature of modern science had been born" (31).

8. See Ernan McMullin, "Introduction: The Concept of Matter in Transition," in *The Concept of Matter in Modern Philosophy*, ed. E. McMullin (Notre Dame, IN: University of Notre Dame Press, 1978), 1–55, here 18–19.

9. And yet all three of these terms were used to describe the substance of spirits, souls, and demons by Greeks, Jews, and Christians.

10. See R. Renehan, "On the Greek Origins of the Concepts of Incorporeality and

post-resurrection appearances in Luke's and John's descriptions and Paul's (sometimes cryptic and quite terse) assertions about resurrection bodies, however, are anything but incorporeal and immaterial. The resurrection in Luke, John, and Paul is *sōma*, not *asōmatos*.

Ernan McMullin once noted for the ancient worldview, "The human spirit was regarded as somehow different from the body it inhabits; belief in survival after death often involved some sort of dualism of the kind. *But categories for describing this contrast were lacking;* the spirit was taken to be a sort of finer material, no more."[11] The fact that the Apostles could so easily identify Jesus' post-resurrection appearance as that of "a spirit" appearing to them, despite the obvious physicality of Jesus' appearance (see Luke 24:37–39) illustrates in a most profound way McMullin's observation that clear categories for distinguishing a contrast between a spirit body and a human body were often lacking in the ancient world. From the Lukan account, human bodies and spirit bodies, apparently, looked too much alike for there to have been a way to clearly demarcate between physical and spiritual. Furthermore, the fact that Jesus' fully physical post-resurrection appearance, with all of the material evidence for it (see John 20:24–27), that was initially construed by the Apostles as "a spirit" suggests that spirits could, indeed, appear in a physical form. We are forced to conclude that calling a spirit (or a soul) "bodiless" or even "incorporeal" did not necessarily mean "immaterial" or "nonphysical" for the ancient worldview as it does today. For all intents and purposes a body for the ancient worldview was the everyday physical body that slept, worked, ate, bathed, bled, sang, and became sick, died, and decayed. So from this perspective a spirit (or a soul) would have been bodiless only in the sense that it lacked *this* kind of body (a *sōma*), not that it lacked *a* body (which Paul, too, called *sōma*).[12] The invisibility (*aoratō*) of spirits may have been a possible impetus for the ancient notion of a spirit's incorporeality, but upon closer inspection a spirit's invisibility did not mean that it lacked a body.[13]

Immateriality," *Greek, Roman, and Byzantine Studies* 21 (1980): 105–38, here 135.

11. So Ernan McMullin, "Introduction: The Concept of Matter," in *The Concept of Matter* (Notre Dame, IN: University of Notre Dame Press, 1963), 1–41, here 15 (italics mine).

12. See Dale Martin, *The Corinthian Body* (New Haven, CT: Yale University Press, 1995), 3–37, 115–7, 127–8.

13. So Jean-Pierre Vernant, "Mortals and Immortals: The Body of the Divine," in *Mortals and Immortals: Collected Essays of Jean-Pierre Vernant* , ed. F. Zeitlin (Princeton, NJ: Princeton University Press, 1991), 27–49, who states, "The gods, therefore, have a

Jesus' Post-Resurrection Appearances

In essence, we are faced with a kind of two-body theory: the corruptible human body and the incorruptible spirit body. Their relationship and "connection" to one another has long baffled philosophers, theologians, and scientists alike.[14] The physical descriptions of Jesus' resurrection appearances in the Gospels compelled early Christian writers to defend a position that sought refuge in a single-body theory, the resurrection of the flesh. For instance, Justin Martyr could not understand a "body" apart from that which was purely physical:

> If the resurrection were only spiritual, it was requisite that He, in raising the dead, should show the body lying apart by itself, and the soul living apart by itself. But now He did not do so, but raised the body, confirming in it the promise of life.[15]

Justin is one of our earliest post-apostolic apologetic sources for the doctrine of the "resurrection of the flesh" even though that phrase does not occur in the New Testament. Justin's identification of Jesus' resurrecting others with Jesus' own resurrection though misses one important point: Jesus is called "the *first* born of the dead" (1 Cor 15:20; Col 1:8). By this reckoning Jesus' resurrection must mean something other than those who had been physically raised by him prior to his own resurrection.[16] Furthermore, in cases like Lazarus and Jairus' daughter it might be more apropos to speak of physical resuscitation rather than resurrection.

---

body that they can at will make (or keep) totally invisible to mortal eyes—and it does not cease to be a body" (42).

14. The modern term for this problem is the mind-body problem, a problem that originates in Descartes' *Meditations*: How is an immaterial unextended thing connected to a material extended body?

15. *On the Resurrection*, 9 (*ANF* 1.298). Interestingly, Justin shared more with the Greek atomists such as the Epicureans who believed all reality to be made up of matter, than with the more spiritual theories of other Greek thinkers, namely Pythagoras and Plato.

16. Note the inherent problem in Matt 27:52–53: "tombs were opened, and the bodies of many saints who had fallen asleep were raised. And coming forth from their tombs after (*meta*) his resurrection, they entered the holy city and appeared to many." The word *meta*, "after," had to be inserted or else Jesus' status as "*first*-born of the dead" would have been canceled out. This means that these bodies would have been laid out of the tombs for three days until Jesus' resurrection had already occurred. But during this three-day interim period, wouldn't they have been reburied? Furthermore, is this what was meant by resurrection of the dead, the physical, corruptible body in the tomb is raised, as these verses suggest? Not, at least, in Paul, as we shall see below.

The two-body doctrine is shared by many ancient folk, including Egyptians,[17] Hebrews,[18] Greeks,[19] and Romans.[20] In our day and age, the two-body theory is dramatically illustrated in spirit materializations whereby a deceased person appears as a fully-formed human being while their deceased physical remains lay buried in a cemetery. So let us look to first-century sources for the two-body theory that will aid in our understanding of Jesus' post-resurrection appearances to his followers in tandem with modern reports on spirit materializations that will aid in "reconciling" (or better: explaining) what appears to be a clash between Lukan and Johannine reports of a physical resurrection and Paul's polemical assertions about a non-physical resurrection.

Richard C. Carrier provides a study of the two-body doctrine as it occurred in first-century Judaism.[21] Carrier notes that while the popular Jewish ideology distinguished between body and soul, almost to the point that one may come away with the notion that early Jews distinguished between a corporeal human body and an incorporeal soul, the descriptions in Philo and Josephus tend to support a (some kind of) bodily soul. Carrier shows that for Philo the physical body is merely a corruptible prison for the soul, a body that "took its substance from the earth, and is again dissolved into the earth" (Philo, *On the Migration of Abraham*, 2–3). The soul departs "from the mortal body and returns as if to the mother-city" (Philo, *Questions and Answers on Genesis*, 3.11). This soul, however, like the angels, is a substance that is *pneumatikos*, "spiritual." For this reason, angels in the past could take the form of men to procreate with women (Philo, *Questions and Answers on Genesis*, 1.92). Carrier concludes that although lacking an earthly mortal body, departed souls still have substance, and in a sense have a different

---

17. See Renahan, "On the Greek Origins," 105.

18. See John W. Cooper, *Body, Soul, and Life Everlasting: Biblical Anthropology and the Monism-Dualism Debate* (Grand Rapids, MI: Eerdmans, 1989), "Any Israelite would agree nevertheless that the 'self' or 'life' in Sheol lacks flesh and bones. So *nephesh* would connote discarnate persons even if it did not denote them. These considerations have led some scholars to conclude that *nephesh* is occasionally used to refer to a personal being which survives physical death and remains in existence" (61).

19. See John P. Wright and Paul Potter, eds., *Psyche and Soma: Physicians and Metaphysicians on the Mind-Body Problem from Antiquity to Enlightenment* (New York: Oxford University Press, 2002), 37–56.

20. See Cicero, *Republic* 6.24.

21. Richard C. Carrier, "The Spiritual Body of Christ and the Legend of the Empty Tomb," in *The Empty Tomb: Jesus Beyond the Grave*, ed. R. Price and J. Lowder (Amherst, NY: Prometheus, 2005), 105–231.

kind of body: "the soul is in effect its own body, made of 'ether,' but at birth this body is sent into the earthly body that is subject to death and decay."[22]

Like Philo, Josephus describes the human body as a prison for the soul (Josephus, *Jewish Wars*, 2.154–5). As a Pharisee, Josephus believed in the resurrection of the soul and records the Pharisaic belief: "The Pharisees say though every soul is incorruptible, only that of good men crosses over into another body" (Josephus, *Jewish Wars*, 2.163). For Carrier, this is clearly a two-body doctrine: "Josephus could not be any clearer: he says that in the resurrection our soul will 'cross over' (*metabainein*) into 'a different body' (*eis heteron sōma*)."[23] Elsewhere, Carrier cites Josephus in another example for a two-body doctrine, namely *Jewish Wars*, 3.372, 374–5, in which "Josephus clearly asserts that in the resurrection we will get *new* bodies, not the same 'corruptible' ones we once had."[24]

This two-body doctrine is found elsewhere beyond Philo and Josephus. Cicero expresses a similar belief in his *Republic* 6.24: "For that man whom your outward form reveals is not yourself; the spirit is the true self, not the physical figure which can be pointed out by the finger." The Christian Gnostic text *Treatise on Resurrection* (or *Letter to Rheginos*) says of the two bodies that "the visible members which are dead shall not be saved [but] the living members which exist within them shall arise" (47.30–48.6). This is not a "Gnostic" heresy as some scholars like to argue, for we see the very same idea in Cicero who wrote in Latin during the first century BCE. The "*visible* members" refer to the members of the physical body; the "*living* members which exist within" the physical members refer to the members of the spirit body.

When we read 1 Cor 15:35–58, we see clearly that resurrected individuals have bodies: "what kind of body (*sōma*) will they come with?" Carrier notes that Paul's response to this question in 1 Cor 15:36–38 illustrates that Paul is reprimanding the Corinthians "for not understanding that there are *two bodies*, in effect one that ages and bleeds to death, and another, 'the body that will come to be.'"[25] In short, Paul believed that the resurrection body, "the new body," would be constituted not of flesh, but *pneuma*.

Paul's resurrection body is corporeal (*sōma*) yet imperishable (*phthora*), which must have sounded oxymoronic to Greeks because the word

---

22. Carrier, "Spiritual Body," 112.
23. Carrier, "Spiritual Body," 112.
24. Carrier, "Spiritual Body," 113 (emphasis his).
25. Carrier, "Spiritual Body," 122 (emphasis his).

sōma was a term for the very body that does perish at death: the human physical body that bleeds, ages, and then dies. And yet Paul does not argue that the resurrection body is the same body that once hung on the cross bloodied, mangled, and punctured, and has now been changed into something else.[26] Note that whereas later Christian apologists believed that the flesh would be raised, e.g. Justin, "the resurrection is a resurrection of the flesh which died" (*On the Resurrection* 10; and see above), and Tertullian (*On the Resurrection of the Flesh*), Paul never says that the *sarx* is raised. Quite the contrary, "flesh (*sarx*) and blood (*haima*) are not received into the kingdom of God" (1 Cor 15:50).

When Paul talks about the resurrection body, he does so by contrasting *sōma pneumatikon*, "body of a spirit," with *sōma psuchikon*, "body of a living physical thing" (1 Cor 15:44). Initially, one is struck by an argument that *contrasts* two qualifiers, namely *pneumatikon* ("spiritual") and *psuchikon* ("soulish") that are otherwise usually understood as referring to the *same* category of reality by the ancients: an "ethereal" reality or a reality of "subtle substance." The English terms "demons," "angels," "spirits," "ghosts," "souls," and "apparitions" are meanings for both *pneuma* and *psuche* in classical and biblical literature. Thus, if we didn't have a particularly clear context, as we do in 1 Cor 15:35–58, then one might assume that the *sōma pneumatikon* and the *sōma psuchikon* both referred to a subtle body, the body of a spirit or the body of a soul. Paul's context, however, prevents us from assuming an identity of this kind between *pneumatikon* and *psuchikon*: he contrasts corruptible, terrestrial, and *psuchikon* bodies with incorruptible, celestial, and *pneumatikon* bodies. The upshot is that the *sōma psuchikon* "is doomed to destruction, because [it] is *psychikon*, a body defined by worldly passions, earthly substance, animal nature, and attachment to this life, and therefore fundamentally corruptible. This body, the body of the flesh [the *psuchikon* body], dies and does not return."[27]

---

26. See Carrier, "Spiritual Body," 123: "To speak of *changing* the *same* body would be far more likely if it was indeed the same body Jesus had when he rose from the grave. Yet that is not the argument Paul makes" (emphasis his).

27. Carrier, "Spiritual Body," 132. I am particularly partial to Carrier's exegesis on this point. He explains: "In the Pauline corpus, *pneumatikos* is routinely contrasted with physical things, like labor, money, food, drink, rocks, human bodies (*sarkinos*), and 'flesh and blood' (*haima kai sarka*). So when *psychikos* is contrasted with it, Paul certainly has in mind something physical, representing the very same contrast. For a *psychikon* is everything a *pneumatikon* is not. And above all things a *pneumatikon* is not made of flesh, therefore a *psychikon* must be. In 1 Corinthians 15, Paul only mentions two bodies, and if one of them, just like all pneumatic things, is not flesh, it follows necessarily that the

In light of the two-body doctrine, however, 1 Corinthians 15:51–54 pose some confusion. When Paul writes "we shall all be changed" (v. 51) and "that which is corruptible must clothe itself with incorruptibility, and that which is mortal must clothe itself with immortality" (vv. 53–54), it sounds as if Paul is suggesting that the physical body somehow participates in the resurrection event. The verb he uses in v. 51, *allagēsometha* comes from *alassō* which means "to change" or "to alter," but in the sense of "exchanging" one thing for another, e.g. change clothes, change appearance.[28] This sense helps us understand Paul's exchange-of-clothing metaphor in vv. 53–54. Paul describes this *allagēsometha*, this "exchange," by saying that the corruptible body will be "clothed" (*endusasthai*). The verb *endusasthai* comes from *enduō* which means "to put on" or more literally, "to go into," as in for getting into clothes. But if this clothing affects an exchange of one thing for another, then how does something corruptible become something incorruptible by putting on a coat? Paul's clothing metaphor makes sense only if we read it in terms of the exchange mentioned in v. 51. Carrier puts it this way: "How would dirt putting on a coat make it no longer dirt? But on the theory that our bodies will be traded in ['exchanged'] we can make sense of the metaphor: as the mortal body enters the realm of the imperishable, and is enveloped by it, it passes away, leaving on the imperishable garment, without which we would perish entirely."[29] Compare this with what Paul writes in 2 Cor 5:1–8, "For we know that if our earthly dwelling, a tent, should be destroyed, we have a building from God, a dwelling not made with hands, eternal in heaven. For in this tent we groan, longing to be further clothed with our heavenly habitation if indeed, when we have taken it off, we shall not be found naked. For while we are in this tent we groan and are weighed down, because we do not wish to be unclothed but to be further clothed, so that what is mortal may be swallowed up by life. . . .

---

other one, the only other body there is, must be flesh," i.e. the *psuchikon* body (128–9). See the versions that render *sōma psuchikon* in the following ways: "a natural body" (NIV, NLT, NAB, KJV), and "a physical body" (International Standard Version, God's Word). So Carrier, "Thus the body without a *psyche* is [physically] dead, a body with a *psyche* is [physically] alive. But more importantly, Adam's body is made of earth ('dirt' as Paul says). In contrast, Christ's [resurrection] body is not. It comes from heaven, not earth, and is a spirit, not a body, at least not in the sense that Adam had a body heaped up for him from the dirt. Insofar as the risen Christ has a body, it is made of *pneuma* from heaven, not earth" (134).

28. See Carrier, "Spiritual Body," 136.
29. Carrier, "Spiritual Body," 137.

although we know that while we are at home in the body we are away from the Lord, . . . and we would rather leave the body and go home to the Lord."

Two things should be noted here. Firstly, the notion that "we shall not be found naked" means that "we shall not be without a body" even though we have taken "it off," i.e. the physical, corruptible body of flesh and blood that Paul calls "a tent" and says in 1 Cor 15:50 cannot be received into heaven. Secondly, Paul's talk of "leaving the body" in order to go home to the Lord is a phenomenon that Paul actually records himself experiencing (in the third person) in 2 Cor 12:1-4, but here it is only a temporary journey out of his physical body to "the third heaven;" otherwise, Paul returns to his physical body and is able to tell the tale fourteen years later. I argue that what Paul could not determine was either "in" or "out" of the [physical] body was, in fact, the spirit body, or as Cicero might put it, Paul's "true self." Carrier becomes confused on this point:

> Paul had no clear idea of how someone could be in any location at all without a body, yet a normal human body cannot enter heaven. If this man he knew had gone to heaven bodily, he would have to have been given a spiritual body, which would all but constitute a resurrection before the last trumpet, thus contradicting Paul's own doctrine, and making no sense of the fact that he came back into his old body again afterward (which leaves open the question of where his new heavenly body then went, if it is supposed to be imperishable).[30]

But there is no contradiction here if we take into account that a part of the psychology of the ancient worldview held that certain people had the ability to temporarily transcend their physical body in the form of a soul or a spirit (even before Christ's resurrection), travel into the beyond, and then return to the physical body. An out-of-body experience is dependent on the physical body being present to receive, once again, the spirit body on its return from journeys into the beyond. The resurrection, however, is not dependent on the physical body. The spirit body does not return to reanimate the physical body as in the cases of out-of-body experiences. The spirit body is resurrected, not the physical body. The spirit body is not waiting in heaven to be put on at some future date by whatever it is that leaves the physical body immediately at death. The spirit body is temporarily housed in the physical body until the physical body dies. Paul's "tent" metaphor suggests that the "I" resides in the dwelling of a physical body,

---

30. Carrier, "Spiritual Body," 153.

Jesus' Post-Resurrection Appearances

the "Me." The "I" is the spirit body; the "Me" is the physical body, the "tent" that is discarded at death. Once the "I" has discarded its tent, the "I" *puts on* incorruptibility and immortality, i.e. *it is free of* the corruptible and mortal tent in which it was once housed.[31] Although Paul's lingo "at the last trumpet" sounds eschatological, we are probably on more sound footing to read that lingo along with the two phrases that precede it than reading it in an eschatological (end of the world; final day of judgment) context. Paul's describing the resurrection event as occurring "in an instant, in the blink of an eye, at the last trumpet" (1 Cor 15:52) refers to the separation of the spirit body from the physical body *at the moment* of physical death. Many near-death experiencers who have been clinically dead and who are revived describe leaving their physical body as instantaneous.[32]

When we read the Lukan and Johannine reports of Jesus' post-resurrection appearance to the Apostles, it seems as if the empty tomb can be explained in this way: the crucified and entombed body of Jesus somehow left the tomb, wounds and all, and appeared before the Apostles. The Lukan passage is often used in support of this: "While they were still speaking about this, he stood in their midst and said to them, 'Peace be with you.' But they were startled and terrified and thought that they were seeing a spirit. Then he said to them, 'Why are you troubled? And why do questions arise in your hearts? Look at my hands and my feet, that it is I myself. Touch me and see, because a spirit does not have flesh and bones as you can see I have.' And as he said this, he showed them his hands and his feet" (Luke 24:36–40). The Johannine passage is even more explicit for the physicality of Jesus' post-resurrection appearance: "But he [Thomas] said to them, 'Unless I see the mark of the nails in his hands and put my finger

---

31. This phenomenon is sometimes described as entering "into another body" as Josephus put it, *eis heteron sōma*. What seems to be the case, at least in the Pauline sense, is that the spirit body "enters into incorruptibility," i.e. it leaves the habitation of the corruptibility of the physical body and is now a spirit body free of the mortal clothing that once bound it.

32. By invoking the near-death experience in order to explain a part of Paul's lingo for resurrection, I am not mixing up what I had earlier clearly distinguished: resuscitations and resurrection. Resuscitation has to do with physical bodies whereas resurrection has to do with spirit bodies. Whereas near-death experiencers are resuscitated, their experience of leaving behind the physical body that has, for a time, died, is nevertheless the same phenomenon that occurs when permanent physical death occurs: the spirit body exits the physical body, never to return to it again. Near-death experiences are, in fact, out-of-body experiences with the added dimension of a "forced" exit from the body due to death unlike out-of-body experiences that are accomplished through meditation or altered states of consciousness by an otherwise healthy person (see 2 Cor 12:1–4).

into the nailmarks and put my hand into his side, I will not believe.' Now a week later his disciples were again inside and Thomas was with them. Jesus came, although the doors were locked, and stood in their midst and said, 'Put your finger here and see my hands, and bring your hand and put it into my side, and do not be unbelieving, but believe" (John 20:25–27). A part of the Lukan report agrees with Paul's polemic on the resurrection body: just as a spirit does not have flesh and bones, so too the body of a spirit (*sōma pneumatikon*) lacks flesh and blood because such cannot be received into the kingdom of God. And so if we are willing to contend that the concept of resurrection is what Paul says it is, then we need to deal with the physicality of Luke's and John's reports of Jesus' post-resurrection appearances in the light of Paul's two-body doctrine for the resurrection.[33]

At this point, it becomes necessary to introduce spirit materializations into the discussion. Spirit materialization, a little-known phenomenon, is not easy to define, but we can initially say that it involves the appearance or the creation of matter from unknown sources. This matter takes on the shape of the spirit's body so that the invisible spirit may become visible to a human being. Spirit materializations were experienced at sittings for spirit communication during the late nineteenth and early twentieth centuries in both Europe and America. Notwithstanding the possibility of fraud, some materializations were examined by trained scientists who concluded that out of thin air a fully functional human being had formed before their eyes, *in broad day light and not in a semi-dark room*, and now stood before them, breathing and speaking in a normal tone of voice.

One of the most dramatic examples of these full-bodied day-light materializations occurred during the early part of the twentieth century in São Paulo, Brazil. The sources from which spirits take on matter in order to become visible to human beings are sometimes human beings themselves, in this case, those who are called "materialization mediums." Those experienced in this field explain that such mediums liberate a part of their

---

33. For instance, Carrier believes that Luke and Paul *do not* agree whatsoever on the nature of the resurrection body: "Though Paul would certainly agree that a spirit does not have flesh and bones, since those are of the dust of the earth, and thus perishable, he could not possibly have believed that the risen Jesus was composed of flesh and bones. For Paul says such things are perishable, and they cannot enter heaven, so they cannot have any place in the resurrection. And he clearly says, contrary to Luke, that the risen Christ *is* a spirit. Nor can Christ's resurrection-body have had blemishes like wounds, since that contradicts Paul's teaching that the raised body is glorious, indestructible, and not made of flesh. . . . We can therefore reject all the Gospel material emphasizing the physicality of Christ's resurrection as a polemical invention" (135, emphasis his).

physical vitality during an altered state of consciousness in order to affect materialization of a spirit. One such medium was a Brazilian of Italian parentage, namely Carlos Mirabelli (1889–1951). A report of Mirabelli's materializations was made in a German journal devoted to the study of paranormal phenomena.[34] There we read of the appearance of spirits in bodily form that were handled by the spectators present for the event. During one materialization

> the shape of a girl appeared beside the medium. Quite shocked, her father, Dr. de Souza, stepped out of the circle, spoke to his child, went close to her and folded her in his arms. Amid convulsive sobs he assured the others again and again that it was his own daughter whom he was holding, and that the dress worn by the apparition was the same as that in which she had been buried.... Colonel Octavio Viana now rose to convince himself of the reality of the apparition. He also took the child in his arms, felt of her pulse, looked into her deep, fathomless eyes, and asked her several questions, which she answered rationally. Viana also was able to confirm that the vision was tangible.[35]

Another report in the same article reads as follows:

> The presence in the room of the figure of Bishop Jose de Camargo Barros appeared, who had lost his life when the ship 'Syrio' was wrecked. Mirabelli was put under the prescribed supervision, conducted this time by Ataliba de Aranha and Odassio Sampaio. As the medium passed into a trance, the scent of roses filled the room. Suddenly there appeared within the circle a fine mist on which everyone present was anxiously observing. The mist parted and became denser, glowing like a gold cloud, out of which gradually, little by little, emerged a smiling apparition wearing the episcopal biretta while clad in the full regalia of church office. As it arose from a chair it announced its name: 'Dr. Jose de Camargo Barros,' in a clear voice which all could hear. Dr. Ganymed de Souza, without any fear, approached the materialized spirit, face to face with it. The apparition smiled silently at the investigator, who now went closer to it, touching and examining it in detail by tapping its body and teeth and rubbing his finger over the gums to determine the

---

34. See "Carlos Mirabelli, das neue brasilianische Medium," *Zeitschrift fuer Parapsychologie* 2 (1927): 449–62. Online: <http://dl.ub.uni-freiburg.de/diglit/zs_para_ga>. For a more recent treatment of Mirabelli, see Guy Lion Playfair, *The Flying Cow: Exploring the Psychic World of Brazil* (Guildford: White Crow, 2011), 23–50.

35. "Carlos Mirabelli," 458 (translation mine).

presence of any saliva. He listened to the heart and to the breathing. He put his ear to the stomach to assure himself that the bowels were functioning. He observed the finger nails and the eyes, and gave close attention to the veins of the eyes, and then resumed his seat. There was no skepticism in his mind, no question whatsoever that the figure before him was that of a man.[36]

Photographs were also taken of Mirabelli's materializations. One was of the materialization of the eighteenth-century Italian poet Giuseppi Parini (1729–1799) taken at the Cesar Lombroso Academy of Psychic Studies in Brazil. In the photograph Mirabelli is seated to the right of Parini, and an observer, Dr. Carlos de Castro, is seated to the left of Parini. Parini is wearing period dress and a pair of spectacles. As a materialized spirit, Parini looks to all outward appearances to be one of the sitters themselves, i.e. he looks to be a normal human being. This photograph is available to anyone's inspection on the internet via a search in Google.

Another variety of spirit materialization was exhibited by the Warsaw medium Franek Kluski (1874–1949). A report of the materializations in his presence was made.[37] The manifesting spirits were given the opportunity to make molds of complex hand folds out of hot paraffin wax. Pictures were made of these molds and they show detailed skin surfaces, nails and cuticles, knuckles, and wrinkles. Kluski's spectators could hear the splashing of the hot paraffin wax as soon as the spirit thrust its hands into the wax. These molds suggest that the wax coated the very shape of the spirit's hands themselves, indicating that a spirit in his or her spiritual environment or dimension possesses hands that look like that of normal human hands. The paraffin wax reveals the form and shape of the hand of *a spirit*.[38]

If Mirabelli's and Kluski's materializations were those of actual spirits, then such phenomena show that the material stuff which clothes the spirit actually reveals the shape and form of the spirit itself, just as it looks and exists in the spiritual dimension. A crude and imperfect analogy might be the impression made by a coin that has been placed under a sheet of notebook paper upon which an impression of the coin's face is left behind when a pencil is rubbed on the very spot of the paper under which the coin is

---

36. "Carlos Mirabelli," 459–60 (translation mine).

37. See F. W. Pawlowski, "The Mediumship of Franek Kluski of Warsaw," *Journal of the American Society for Psychical Research* 19 (1925): 481–504.

38. See Pawlowski, "Mediumship," 488–98. Pictures of these molds can be seen in Pawlowski, "Mediumship," 489–96.

located. The impression left on the paper is made by graphite particles of the pencil. These graphite particles, in and of themselves, do not possess the shape of the coin. Rather, the graphite particles reveal the shape of the coin in question, a shape that already exists even before the impression is ever made. So, too, with spirit materializations.

When we now read Luke 24:36–40 and John 20:24–27 in the light of both Paul's two-body doctrine of the resurrection and modern reports of spirit materializations, we can explain the astonishment and fear of the Apostles and the physicality of Jesus' post-resurrection appearances. Those experienced with spirit materializations are familiar with the fact that a spirit who wants to be recognized by friends and acquaintances will appear to them in a form that marks the spirit as the very person the friends and acquaintances knew in life. For instance, Gambier Bolton remarks in his study of spirit materializations, "We are told that, *for the purpose of identification*, the entity will return to earth in an exact counterpart of the body which he alleges that he occupied at the time of his death, and *in order that he may be recognized* by his relatives and friends who happen to be present."[39] By exhibiting his wounds and his body as it looked entombed, Jesus, as a spirit, was manifesting in a way that the disciples would *recognize him* in order to calm their fears (see Luke 24:37), rid their doubt (see John 20:27), and convince them of life after death. The scars of Jesus that doubting Thomas examined were such an appearance so that Thomas could easily recognize his Master. Otherwise, if Jesus manifested to them in the way that he manifested to Paul on the road to Damascus, in a great celestial form of bright, white light, then would the disciples have recognized their Master?[40]

---

39. Gambier Bolton, *Ghosts in Solid Form: An Experimental Investigation of Certain Little-Known Phenomena (Materializations)* (London: William Rider & Son, 1916; 3rd ed., 1919), 31 (emphasis mine).

40. Recall that Jesus was not always recognized during his post-resurrection appearances. We see in both early and later appearances of the post-resurrection pre-ascension Jesus that the scars and wounds no longer appear on his body. Once spirits are recognized, then, on some occasions they will appear later in a healthier form if they initially appeared sickly or aged in order to be recognized. See Bolton (ibid.), "One who left the earth as an infant will appear in his materialized body as an infant, although he may have been dead for twenty or thirty years. The aged man or woman will appear with bent body, wrinkled face, and snow-white hair, walking amongst us with difficulty, and just as they allege they did before their death, although that may have occurred twenty years before. The one who had lost a limb during his earth-life will return minus that limb; the one who was disfigured by accident or disease will return bearing distinct traces of that disfigurement, for the purpose of identification only. But as soon as the identification has been established successfully, all this changes instantly: the disfigurement disappears:

If we evaluate and consider the records in our own day of the materialization of spirit bodies and those who examined these materialized bodies as bodies that looked, felt, and acted like normal people, then from this data the mystery of Jesus' resurrection body is immediately solved: contrary to what some scholars argue (see n. 33 above), there is no discontinuity between the "spiritual" Pauline resurrection account and the "physical" Lukan and Johannine resurrection accounts—the resurrected Jesus is a spirit, supported by the assertions that he is "a life-giving spirit" and "flesh and blood cannot inherit the kingdom of God" (1 Cor 15:45, 50), and the resurrected Jesus *as a materialized spirit* is physical to all outward appearances during his post-resurrection stay on earth (Luke 24:39 and John 20:20, 27).

But does any of this explain the empty tomb? Since no medium was present, or necessary in the case of Jesus' materialization we might speculate that Jesus' own physical body that had been entombed was the source from which matter was liberated and used to make his spirit body visible to the Apostles. This could very well explain why the body was no longer present. The fact that the tomb was empty upon its discovery by Mary Magdalene and Peter three days after the crucifixion has suggested to many that the body that was hanging on the cross was the same body that walked out of the tomb. But the physical body does not resurrect (1 Cor 15:50), and the resurrection is not a resuscitation as it would have been if Jesus' physical body had awoken and walked out. The resurrection body is the body of *a spirit* (1 Cor 15:45) and not the body of *a human being* (1 Cor 15:44). Just as a portion of a materialization medium's physical vitality is said to be "dissolved" in order to be liberated from him or her to be used to materialize a spirit close by, it is not impossible to speculate that something similar happened to Jesus' physical body. Philo says that salvation requires abandoning the physical body, "because the body took its substance from the earth, and is again *dissolved* into the earth" (*On the Migration of Abraham* 2–3). The body, according to Philo, will dissolve into the four elements of which it was made, "but the mental and celestial species of the soul will depart into the purest ether" which Philo says is a fifth substance superior to the other four of which the body is made, and this 'ether' is the stuff of which "the stars and the whole heaven" are made, as well as the human soul (*Who*

---

the four limbs will be seen, and both the infant and the aged will from henceforth show themselves to us in the very prime of life—the young growing upwards and the aged downwards, as we say, and, as they one and all state emphatically, just as they really look and feel in the sphere in which they now exist" (31–32).

is the Heir of Divine Things 283).[41] Whereas all physical bodies *gradually* dissolve through the process known as "decay," Christ's physical body was not meant to see "corruption" (Psalm 16:10; Acts 2:31). His body dissolved, but not through decay. Hence, we may wonder if it was dissolved by some divine action in order to build up Jesus' materialized spirit body.[42]

If the resurrection is the resurrection of a spirit body, then the notion that "the resurrection of the dead" refers to the resurrection of dead physical bodies buried in cemeteries needs to be reassessed. In other words "the dead" here means something other than dead human bodies. In a biblical sense, death and dead often mean "separation" as in the Pauline phrase "dead to sin," i.e. separated from sin. In the parable of the rich man and Lazarus (Luke 16:19–31), the rich man dies and is buried but he nevertheless remains conscious "in Hades" (v. 23). While in Hades, he is separated from God by "a great chasm" (v. 26). The rich man's place of confinement in Hades is actually called "the dead" (vv. 30, 31). Even though the rich man's body had been buried, he remained aware and conscious of his plight among "the dead" in Hades, i.e. among those separated from God. So "the dead" in this case are not the unconscious physical bodies decaying in the ground; the dead are those in Hades separated from their physical bodies yet remaining conscious apparently in another body that speaks, sees, and hears.

Another clue as to the meaning of "the dead" might be found in Heb 2:14, "him who holds the power of death, that is, the devil." In the Jewish and Christian tradition, God's greatest antagonist is labeled by many names, e.g. the serpent, Satan, Beelzebub, Death, and the Devil. Here we see that the "power of death" is none other than a power to separate individuals from

---

41. Note, too, that Paul speaks of the resurrection body in similar ways: "There are both heavenly (celestial) bodies and earthly (terrestrial) bodies, but the brightness of the heavenly is one kind and that of the earthly another. The brightness of the sun is one kind, the brightness of the moon another, and the brightness of the stars another. For star differs from star in brightness. So also is the resurrection of the dead" (1 Cor 15:40–42). On the resurrection body as a celestial body like stars, see Alan Scott, *Origen and the Life of Stars: A History of an Idea* (Oxford: Clarendon, 1991, repr. 2001), 150–64.

42. Allison (*Resurrecting Jesus*) rehearses several hypotheses to explain Jesus' empty tomb and resurrection appearances. One hypothesis is the disintegration of Jesus' physical body while in the tomb: "The body remained where Joseph of Arimathea laid it, but its disintegration was so rapid that, when the tomb was entered shortly after Jesus' interment, it appeared that its occupant had vanished" (212). Allison dismisses this hypothesis as "hocus-pocus" and regards it as a thesis "of ingenuity over good sense" (212). Allison quotes others who support such a thesis, but none of them explain the disintegration of Jesus' body with the purpose of materializing his spirit body, which the two-body theory helps explain (213 n. 59).

God, in the same way as we see the rich man in the Lukan parable. Those who are God-fearing are not dead while those who do not have God in their lives are considered "dead." This is the very point made in 1 Tim 5:5–6, "The real widow, who is all alone, has set her hope on God and continues in supplications and prayers night and day. But the one who is self-indulgent is dead while she [physically] lives." Dead in this sense is estrangement or divorce from God. So we may speak of physical death as a separation of the spirit body from the physical body and spiritual death as a separation of one from God, whether one is still "housed" in a physical body (as in the case of the widow in 1 Tim 5:6) or has left the physical body through physical death and resides among "the dead" in a spirit dimension, Hades.[43]

Reading "resurrection of the dead" in this light allows us to make sense out of passages that describe Jesus "descending into the lower parts of the earth" (Eph 4:9) and going "to the spirits in prison" (1 Pet 3:18, 19). If these two passages are in reference to going or descending into Hades, then Jesus' "ascending" (Eph 4:9) would make sense only if he "rose up" out of this netherworld region. And the phrase "firstborn from the dead" (Col 1:18) would suggest that Jesus was the first to be able to cross the chasm that Luke writes of in the parable of the rich man. John 3:13 seems to hint at this as well: "No one has ever gone into heaven except the one who came from heaven—the Son of Man." In other words, no person was allowed (for whatever reason) to ascend into heaven, i.e. resurrect from the dead, until Christ had done so.

Bovell's thesis boldly makes the resurrection not as some future event but as something that is taking place already among humans. This is not too far afield from the scriptural record. Even though I have spent time elaborating on Jesus' post-resurrection appearances, there is also something to be said about how allegiance to Christ in this life while on Earth "raises one from the dead," i.e. no longer separated from God. In Col 2:12 the Colossians are told "having been buried with Him in baptism, in which you were also raised up with Him through faith in the working of God, who raised Him from the dead." By having given Christ their allegiance, the Colossians were already viewed as having been raised from the dead, although their

---

43. Separation from God is the real "death." This is the death that humans should fear more so than physical death, as Augustine once said: "The death which men fear is the separation of the soul from the body. The true death, which men do not fear, is the separation of the soul from God" (*en Ps.* 49.2.1 [*ANF* 6.440, n. 3]). We also see the separation of spirit and physical body in James 2:26, "the body without the spirit is [physically] dead."

departure from Earth had not yet taken place. In other words, as Bovell writes, "The privilege of being a Christian believer is to be found enjoying the preliminary phases of divine communion . . . *in this life* . . . by virtue of Jesus' resurrection and ascension." This is a very perceptive and important insight made by Bovell that opens up for us the meaning of "resurrection of the dead" in ways that I have suggested here: even in this life one is no longer considered "dead" if they are committed to God through Christ (1 Tim 5:6). Even in this physical life, one can be "raised from the dead" if one's allegiance is to Christ whose resurrection has made believers' resurrection possible *both here and now and in the hereafter*. Bovell's thesis for resurrection as "already taking place" is a process whereby one comes to know and understand that "No one comes to the Father except through me" (John 14:6). Once the physical body is discarded after physical death, only then can one "be raised" into the heavens for a more full knowledge of Christ.

Postscript

The Bible and Seminary Experience
We Need to Do More for Our Students

Carlos R. Bovell

OFTEN WHEN EVANGELICAL STUDENTS come to realize that inerrancy is not a fruitful way to describe the Bible's authority, they are prevented from revealing their growth in this area to other believers because of various cultural pressures. If the student happens to work with youth, teach Sunday school, lead Bible study or small group, or preach from time to time, they would almost immediately be asked to cease in order that the community's leaders might re-evaluate their suitability for ministry. Changing one's mind about inerrancy in this kind of church environment is no small matter. In any number of Christian communities across the United States, to not subscribe to inerrancy is still stereotyped as tantamount to apostasy.[1] As a result, there are students who are so worried about ostracism that they not only keep their change of mind hidden from co-believers at church, they also feel pressure to keep it from family members and even their spouses.

It falls to evangelical leaders, then, to speak more candidly and frequently with believers about what alternative positions exist for skeptic inerrantists, to discuss with them the strengths and weaknesses of each, even if they themselves find inerrancy satisfactory. Generally speaking, however, evangelical leaders are not in the habit of doing this enough, and when

---

1. As recently as February 2015, *Christianity Today*, the flagship magazine for American Evangelicalism, published a "testimony" entitled, "How I Almost Lost the Bible: Had it not been for the first editor of CT, I likely would have gone the way of liberal scholar Bart Ehrman" by G. A. Thornbury. Thornbury narrates: "I had come within a whisker of losing my faith. But because Henry was a philosopher defending biblical authority, I rallied." Clearly Carl Henry and Bart Ehrman are not the only options. See G. A. Thornbury, "How I Almost Lost the Bible." Online: <http://www.christianitytoday.com/ct/2015/januaryfebruary/how-i-almost-lost-bible.html> (last accessed 2/18/15).

they do, they rarely do so with an abundance of *grace*.² In fact, in my own limited experience, evangelical scholars are still very far from adequately preparing students for the emotional and social upheaval that critical scholarship brings into both personal spirituality and church life. I was first moved to reflect upon and then write about inerrantist culture when I saw seminary classmates rethinking their calls to ministry because, after only basic classes in biblical studies, they began to be concerned that they might be rejected from the ordination process. One of the main sticking points stemmed from their denomination's subscription to inerrancy. Men and women who find themselves in this position need more leaders willing to help them sort through the issues, and not with the agenda of steering them back to inerrancy.

Simply put, too few evangelical scholars and leaders are taking their students' emotional crises seriously. Common responses still include: "Students just aren't familiar with the Chicago Statement, so they don't understand how sensible it is," or, "The students simply aren't familiar enough with the Bible (or church history) to appreciate how inerrancy is the biblical (or historical) position," or, "Secular academia is blindsiding students because they don't possess the (inerrantist) philosophical training they need to identify and confront non-Christian worldviews." Aside from being disparaging, responses such as these do not address the problem I am trying to address.

There are many students who, by doubting inerrancy, enter a spiritual race against time. In my experience, the more time that passes without anyone talking honestly with them about what options remain open to believers disillusioned with inerrancy, the less likely the student in question will continue in the faith. Conversely, the sooner evangelical leaders present something more believable (from the perspective of these students) than inerrancy, the less likely it becomes that they will abandon faith.³ I do not

---

2. Craig Blomberg is a notable exception. Though he encourages students to adopt conservative positions, he remains gracious with those who disagree. See Blomberg, *Can We Still Believe the Bible? An Evangelical Engagement with Contemporary Questions* (Grand Rapids: Brazos, 2014), 222.

3. Interestingly, Blomberg wonders how people can "deconvert" so quickly; they seem to go straight from Fundamentalism to atheism. What he does not seem to grasp is how mediating positions come across to the evangelical mindset as special pleading when they have put so much energy into disallowing "errors" in the Bible. Some believers begin to see, if for the first time, that they really have been protecting the Bible from their own close study of it. Compare S. Young, "Protective Strategies and the Prestige of the 'Academic': A Religious Studies and Practice Theory Redescription of Evangelical

wish to imply, however, that the work needed in evangelical bibliology must be done in a hurry. The spiritual need among churches may be great, but the efforts to redress generations of cultural failure in American Evangelicalism will take time. So what we are contending with really is an interim problem: what should we tell believers who want desperately to know how to understand the Bible's inspiration and authority *now*?

In his response essay, George Brooke is ready to "buy in" to my approach to biblical inspiration and authority. In his view, something *like* my approach is actually required, given what is known of the socio-religious culture that Jesus himself participated in. According to Brooke, my proposals fit well with both the thought world and scribal and hermeneutical practices of the Qumran community, for example. This is a very important point, for if an evangelical doctrine of inspiration is going to prove tenable for students in the 21st century, it will have to be versatile enough to account for both what we ourselves are seeking to do with Scripture today and what believers have been doing with Scripture throughout two thousand years of church history (and not merely what *we* think they *should* have been doing with Scripture).

Richard Briggs is also sympathetic to what I am attempting in my proposals. He laments, however, that I chose to begin with a conservative evangelical doctrine of inspiration in the first place. Briggs judges (quite correctly) that I would have been better off had I started somewhere else entirely. However, in God's providence, Fundamentalism is where I came from and out of Fundamentalism is where I am heading. (An unwelcome side effect of having once been a fundamentalist may well be that I will always see myself as still recovering from Fundamentalism.)

Perhaps Briggs is right, then, in his observation that my reading of the fourth Gospel has been shaped by a personal reaction to inerrantism. Notwithstanding, I think the exegetical moves I make are at least broadly Johannine,[4] even if its specific application to an inerrantist, evangelical

---

Inerrantist Scholarship," *Biblical Interpretation* 23 (2015): 1–35. Even Blomberg himself makes clear that evangelicals have to decide how much of the story needs to be history for the Christian narrative to still make sense. Doing scholarship in this way will strike some students as artificial because it deliberately protects the Bible from the results of scholarship. If the Bible needs this kind of saving, and if the faith is constructed as being based on the Bible, then the faith is set up for an imminent collapse.

4. Schneiders, for example, makes similar moves as she looks to the Gospel of John for her portrayal of biblical spirituality as theopoesis. See S. Schneiders, "Biblical Spirituality: Text and Transformation," in *The Bible and Spirituality: Exploratory Essays in Reading Scripture Spiritually*, ed. A. Lincoln, J. G. McConville, and L. Pietersen (Eugene,

doctrine of inspiration arose through my own contexts, both educational and ecclesial. It should be clear either way that I agree with most of what Briggs writes in his chapter. It is reassuring that he reiterated my main points with approval, even presenting them as commonplace ("there is no need to limit inspiration to any one stage of God's superintendence of Scripture"). Yet this is precisely where the differences between my cultural context and that of Briggs come to bear out. The suggestion that readers also are part of the process of inspiring Scripture is a radical one from an American evangelical standpoint. There are plenty who will declare the idea as heterodox or worse.

Mark Mcleod-Harrison has firsthand familiarity with the American evangelical scene. He knows believers who think that their eternal salvation depends upon "getting it right" theologically. Unfortunately, the same mentality is also applied to a believer's doctrine of Scripture. Mcleod-Harrison regrets that believers who put such high stakes on their theological frameworks will have a hard time changing their thinking in the directions I propose. In his chapter, he presents an irrealist metaphysic which maintains that how the world *is*, largely depends on us. The pluralism we see among Christian communities, both today and throughout history, is indicative of how God created the world *to be*. Since believers contribute both to the life of the world *and also to the life of God*, it should come as no surprise that humans alive today contribute as well to the inspiration of Scripture.

From a counseling viewpoint, J. Harold Ellens prefers an experientialist view of Scripture to that of inerrancy. In my account of the Bible's authority, I seek to ground the authority of Scripture subjectively in believers' own experience of Christ and objectively in the experiences of the first Christians when Christ appeared to them after being crucified. Ellens is just as concerned as I am about views of Scripture, and religion for that matter, that, when put in practice, make believers "psychologically sick." Neither he nor I am suggesting that inerrantists, by virtue of being inerrantist, are inherently neurotic (by no means!). Still, it seems safe to say that there can be quite a bit of unhealthy emotional and psychological fallout that comes with incorporating such an extreme view of Scripture as inerrancy into the complexities of twenty-first-century life, especially as informed by American inerrantist culture. Either way, if part of a believer's spiritual healing and growth demands that inerrancy be abandoned, then a commitment to

---

OR: Cascade, 2013), 128–50.

abandoning inerrancy should be commended by all involved, both inerrantists and non-inerrantists alike.

Of all the respondents, Holly Beers was the most critical so I will give more space to commenting on her essay than I did to the others above. Beers agrees with me that inerrantist approaches that rely too heavily on history can become imbalanced. She also acknowledges that, although evangelicals are fond of stating that they are against allegorizing in principle, they appear to be open to it in practice. As an example, she describes how it is not uncommon for evangelicals to allegorize Old Testament narratives in their attempts to derive meaning from them. On the other hand, Beers is cautious about granting allegory/typology too much leeway. She warns that not all readings are equal, but aside from some extreme postmodernist writers, I cannot think of any strand of the Christian tradition which has held that every reading is acceptable. As I mentioned above, even Origen himself complained of other writers who he thought were allegorizing too much. Interestingly enough, remarks like Origen's were typically made when *the results gained* from allegorizing proved objectionable.[5]

Beers goes on to mention a distinction between the hermeneutical practices of the early church fathers and those of the NT writers. She implies that the church fathers' hermeneutics should be viewed as deficient because they failed to acknowledge the Jewishness of Christian Scriptures. This objection seems problematic to me because it would apply not only to the exegesis of the church fathers, East and West, but extend moreover to the entire history of Christian exegesis (up through developments in scholarship that occurred a mere fifty years ago[6]). But more than just a case of chronological snobbery, if Beers is to be followed, then the essential plurality that characterizes the entire gamut of the Christian hermeneutical enterprise needs to be accounted for.[7] Both the church fathers and the NT writers were concerned to show that Jesus' life, death, and resurrection were

---

5. R. Greer, *The Captain of Our Salvation: A Study in the Patristic Exegesis of Hebrews* (Tübingen, Mohr, 1973).

6. J. Charlesworth dates the end of the "Second Quest" at about 1970 but does not see a beginning of the "Third Quest" until about 1980. See Charlesworth, *The Historical Jesus: An Essential Guide* (Nashville, TN: Abingdon, 2008), 7–8.

7. And as I intimate in my essay, distinguishing between Jewish and Hellenistic during this time period is not without difficulty. Compare R. Strelan, *Strange Acts: Studies in the Cultural World of the Acts of the Apostles* (New York: de Gruyter, 2004), 16–18; and M. David Litwa, *Iesus Deus: The Early Christian Depiction of Jesus as a Mediterranean God* (Minneapolis: Fortress, 2014), 6–21.

eschatologically climactic and, as a result, every facet of human existence finds its ultimate purpose in him; this includes the Christian Scriptures.[8]

By contrast, my approach seeks to take the bull by the horns, as it were, by openly acknowledging that the NT's relationship to the OT is loose enough to encourage (and perhaps, actually require) allegorical/typological exegesis. This looseness goes "all the way down" and is not limited to interpretation, but extends to the OT itself: its development in several textual recensions and a variety of canons, each being legitimately accepted by different believing communities without any of them having to be declared exclusively wrong or right. The diachronic history of the OT clearly indicates that Scripture's authority must stem from something other than the fact that it is a component of special revelation per se. This is where Scripture's dynamic spiritual connection to *both* Jesus Christ *and* believers presents itself as a fruitful candidate for establishing Scripture's authority, for, if apart from Jesus Christ, believers can accomplish nothing, then how much more is this true for the Bible!

Beers voices a more serious concern regarding what I say about Christ's resurrection. To be clear, I do believe there is a spirit world.[9] I also believe that the spirit realm is teeming with spiritual beings and that, gradually and ultimately, humans are destined to occupy a spiritual realm too. I regret that Beers found me unclear, but in a way I am not surprised, given my emphasis on visions. There is a history linking such language with a dismissal of the supernatural. For example, when setting down definitions at the beginning of a polemical essay on the resurrection of the body, O'Connell dismisses the idea of *subjective vision* as "synonymous with hallucination."[10] Goulder, who had argued for a vision theory of Jesus' resurrection, famously interpreted visions in a way that left no room for resurrection.[11]

---

8. Froehlich observes how interpretations that did not bear out this assumption were deemed "literal." See K. Froelich, *Sensing the Scriptures: Aminadab's Chariot and the Predicament of Biblical Interpretation* (Grand Rapids: Eerdmans, 2014), 29.

9. That heaven, hell, and purgatory exist, for example. For a Protestant defense of purgatory, see J. Walls, *Heaven, Hell, and Purgatory: Rethinking the Things That Matter Most* (Grand Rapids: Brazos, 2015), 91–116.

10. See J. O'Connell, "Jesus' Resurrection and Collective Hallucinations," *Tyndale Bulletin* 60 (2009): 72.

11. Goulder decided that all visions should be explained (away) naturalistically, categorizing them as "baseless." See M. Goulder, "Baseless Fabric of a Vision," in *Resurrection Reconsidered*, ed. G. D'Costa (Rockport, MA: OneWorld, 1996), 48–61. Contrast I. Stevenson, "The Contribution of Apparitions to the Evidence for Survival," *Journal of the American Society for Psychical Research* 76 (1982): 341–58; J. Pandarakalam, "Are the

For my part, I think something can be said about subjective visions having *objective* components to them. Sparrow, for instance, knows of cases where people are "in the state between waking and sleep where 'reality' mimics the waking state but includes phenomena originating in psychic or spiritual realms."[12] In even deeper trance-like states, the visionaries of Kibeho, for example, were taken on "astral expeditions" by Mary, the mother of Jesus, leaving the physical world behind to visit other spiritual dimensions.[13] So I do affirm Beers' "very real realm of heaven"; I just find it confusing to describe experiences of it as *historical*.[14] To illustrate why, consider the following account of Segatashya of Kibeho's first encounter with the risen Jesus on July 2, 1982:

> I looked upward and suddenly the blue sky above my head parted in the middle like a piece of fabric torn in two. A dazzling light filled the center of the sky. The light was so blinding that everything else around me disappeared in a flash—the people, the farm, the hills and trees, everything vanished. It was very strange because I could still see, but what I was seeing was completely unfamiliar to my eyes. I was in a totally new and different world. I was all alone, standing in a vast sea of vibrant, sweet-smelling, green grass. The light above me grew more brilliant by the second, and then the sky filled with a million shining white flowers, which were more beautiful than you can imagine. A moment later Jesus appeared in the heavens, standing in the midst of the white flowers . . . He was floating high above me . . .[15]

Apparitions of Medjugorje Real?" *Journal of Scientific Exploration* 15 (2001): 229–39; and P. Cunningham, "The Apparition at Medjugorje: A Transpersonal Perspective, Part 1 and 2," *Journal of Transpersonal Psychology* 43 (2011).

12. G. Scott Sparrow, *Blessed among Women: Encounters with Mary and Her Message* (New York: Harmony, 1997), 48.

13. I. Ilibagiza, *Our Lady of Kibeho: Mary Speaks to the World from the Heart of Africa* (New York: Hay House, Inc., 2008), 131.

14. Prince suggests that Luke was trying to ensure that his readers would understand that the disciples' experience of Jesus after he was crucified couldn't be compared with any known post-mortem category known at the time. He did so by narrating events as both consistent *and* inconsistent with every category. See D. Prince, "The 'Ghost' of Jesus: Luke 24 in Light of Ancient Narratives of Post-Mortem Apparitions," *JSNT* 29 (2007): 287–301.

15. I. Ilibagiza, *The Boy Who Met Jesus: Segatashya of Kibeho* (New York: Hay House, Inc., 2011), 80.

Postscript

Given this description, does it seem appropriate to classify Jesus' floating high above Segatashya in some other dimension as *historical*?[16] Segatashya's being transported to a "totally new and different world" is so dissimilar to what we normally regard as historical that it seems confusing at best to regard it in that way. I remain content to term encounters such as these "mystical experiences" or "altered states of consciousness," intending in these cases to affirm both that Segatashya really experienced it *and* that the alternate reality he entered into is somehow "real." In short, I do not deny that Jesus was resurrected nor that he appeared to many of his disciples. I am merely keeping the emphasis where I believe it ought to remain, *on Jesus appearing to people after being crucified.*[17]

Some evangelicals believe that the integrity of the faith depends on convincingly addressing historical difficulties raised by critics.[18] To me, a preoccupation with apologetics can restrict believers' spiritual development.[19] There is an emotional temptation to keep faith aligned with inherited apologetic strategies, but this may not always be helpful.[20] In my essays

---

16. I would not say Segatashya was deluded or hallucinating, nor would I be satisfied with saying that through his experience a new concept for post-mortem existence "stuck." I find it more approximate to say he had an "encounter" experience, though I would hesitate to call it historical. See A. Baxter, "Historical Judgement, Transcendent Perspective and 'Resurrection Appearances,'" *Heythrop Journal* 40 (1999): 19–40.

17. So if, as Robinson suggests, there is a tension in the NT between "luminous" and "bodily" to describe Jesus' resurrection, then I am more than comfortable erring on the side of luminosity. See J. Robinson, "Jesus from Easter to Valentinus (Or the Apostles' Creed)," *JBL* 101 (1982): 5–37.

18. I think Goulder, for example, raises excellent questions that are not easily answered. See M. Goulder, "Jesus' Resurrection and Christian Origins: A Response to N. T. Wright," *Journal for the Study of the Historical Jesus* 3 (2005): 187–95.

19. Our primary focus as believers should always be on purifying our hearts and minds, regularly confessing our sins from our hearts, and changing our lives in repeated attempts to keep us from sinning again. Demonstrating that every gospel pericope is indeed historical can detract from our purification. The danger, as I see it, is that inerrancy convinces students that they can only genuinely attend to the former if they are successful at doing the latter. On this last point, compare W. L. Craig, "What Price Biblical Errancy?" Online: <http://www.reasonablefaith.org/what-price-biblical-errancy> (last accessed 3/27/15).

20. In chapter 5 of *Rehabilitating Inerrancy*, I suggest there are many times when it may be appropriate for students to relax their apologetic concerns. When it comes to apologetics, Beilby observes that "some people have a very high need for reasons [to believe], others have less." My downplaying of apologetics does not make me a fideist. According to Morley, "if you think there is ever any reason to believe, you are not a fideist." See J. Beilby, *Thinking about Christian Apologetics: What It Is and Why We Do*

on biblical authority, I pondered whether the resurrection experiences themselves are sufficient for helping us to better understand, not what Jesus' resurrection might have entailed, but specifically how the experiences could be invoked to support Scripture's authority.[21]

Realizing this, Clint Tibbs decided that he would focus his response essay on the phenomenon of Christ appearing to believers after his crucifixion. In my lead essays, I accepted the traditional position that Christ's appearing to people after being crucified is what convinced the first Christians to uphold his ministry after his death.[22] I went on to suggest that his appearances are also what provide the Bible with its (external) authority today. To explore this further, Tibbs reflects on what kind of "body" is involved when Jesus is said to have appeared to his followers after dying on the cross. He delineates a two-body theory that he finds satisfactory for explaining how Jesus could have died on the cross and been buried for a few days, but nevertheless appeared to believers as alive afterwards.

I am thankful that Tibbs had the courage to write so straightforwardly on the resurrection appearances. Within American Evangelicalism, at least, if the subject of biblical authority is contentious, the topic of Jesus' resurrection is sacrosanct. Unless one has decided ahead of time to maintain the

---

It (Downers Grove, IL: InterVarsity, 2011), 166–7, and B. Morley, *Mapping Apologetics: Comparing Contemporary Approaches* (Downers Grove, IL: InterVarsity, 2015), 351.

21. Or to put it another way, the appearing tradition of 1 Cor 15 is what gives rise to the disappearing tradition of Mark 16; the former's significance should be neither conflated with nor obscured by the latter. Compare van Tilborg and Counet's account of "invisible proof" in Luke 24: "Visibility becomes invisibility and the un-recognized appearance becomes recognized disappearance." Compare also Smith's observation of gradual belief as described, for example, by the Johannine progression "saw and believed." See S. van Tilborg and P. Counet, *Jesus' Appearances and Disappearances in Luke 24* (Boston: Brill, 2000), 84; and D. Smith, *Revisiting the Empty Tomb: The Early History of Easter* (Minneapolis: Fortress, 2010), 143–4.

22. See J. Howell, "ASC Induction Techniques, Spiritual Experiences, and Commitment to New Religious Movements," *Sociology of Religion* 58 (1997): 141–64. Once again, there are plenty of scholars who equate visions with hallucinations. See, for example, H. J. de Jonge, "Visionary Experience and the Historical Origins of Christianity," in *Resurrection in the New Testament: Festschrift J. Lambrecht*, ed. R. Bieringer, V. Koperski and B. Lataire (Dudley, MA: Peeters, 2002), 35–53. But I think this tendency provides a good example of what D. Z. Phillips called "the forgetfulness of religious categories," when researchers overlook how "revelation brings about a dramatic change in behavior, but the change is a change in a person's life. . ." See D. Z. Phillips, "Authority and Revelation," *Archivio di Filosofia* 62 (1994): 685. Compare S. Daily, *Release* (Evesham: Arthur James, n.d.), 10–11.

status quo, exploring the resurrection is unthinkable.²³ Be that as it may, there are times when students can benefit from critically discussing both biblical authority and Jesus' resurrection, particularly if they aim to do so in faith and with good will. And that which can benefit students might also stand to benefit faculty, especially if the questions asked are in the interest of keeping faith alive, for as I once heard a visionary proclaim: "God is not compelling people to believe but calling them to love." So if a different account of the post-resurrection appearances has the potential to re-ignite a person's love for God and humanity, it is more than worth the effort. And honestly, who can say with any assurance that what now, from *an evangelical standpoint*, looks like heretical tampering with fundamental doctrines, might not in the future be recognized as genuinely Christian?

Tibbs decides to broach the topic of the resurrection appearances by asking a simple question, "When an Apostle sees the risen Jesus, what exactly does he see?" He suggests that what the apostles saw may have involved a kind of spiritual materialization. For my part, I agree with Tibbs' instinct that one can profitably consult modern research into spirit phenomena to see if there is a working, conceptual framework available for helping us better understand the NT accounts of resurrection appearances.²⁴ I have long thought that evangelicals are wrong to insist that Jesus' resurrection was so singular in nature that there is nothing like it at all with which it might be compared. At the same time, I would be remiss if I did not explicitly warn students that there is a difference between doing honest research in anthropology, religion, parapsychology, and the like, and getting caught up in

---

23. The resurrection is often presented as non-negotiable, citing Paul's remark that if Christ was not raised then Christians are without hope (see 1 Cor 15.17–19), but perhaps evangelicals are more open to alternate theories than they are often given credit for. Licona, for example, reports that "[m]any evangelical Christians replied that they would not abandon their faith as a result" of archaeological "testing [that] irrefutably demonstrated that these were the bones of Jesus," even though "this would disconfirm the central Christian belief that Jesus was raised." Perhaps they realize that such testing would actually settle for us what manner of resurrection Jesus experienced. An approach to resurrection that focuses on Jesus' *appearances* would still be viable. See M. Licona, *The Resurrection of Jesus: A New Historiographical Approach* (Downers Grove, IL: InterVarsity, 2010), 59–60.

24. See, for example, K. Vincent, "Resurrection Appearances of Jesus as After-Death Communication," *Journal of Near-Death Studies* 30 (2012): 137–48. This volume includes a response essay by evangelical apologist Gary Habermas followed by a rejoinder by Vincent.

(or unwittingly drawn into) personally experimenting or becoming unduly fascinated with the occult and its practices.[25]

That said, it seems to me that the Apostle Paul's remark that what befell Jesus Christ did not happen in a corner also applies to Jesus' post-resurrection appearances. If we understand that Jesus came to show us what possibilities there are for human obedience to God, it stands to reason that most, if not everything, he experienced is patterned after what human beings could all potentially experience. If we press the doctrine of the incarnation to apply also to what happened to Jesus after dying, then perhaps a great deal of what he experienced at death is also a variation of what all humans ordinarily undergo when they die, as opposed to being a singular event that *only* Christ underwent. Or put another way, Jesus was not the only one to be resurrected per se, but he was the only human (i.e., in his human nature) to resurrect *well*, ascending into heaven—with Jesus' human nature going to heaven by virtue of his divine nature returning to heaven after visiting hell to save souls. He was the "first fruit," as the Apostle Paul calls him, the first of the harvest, the first born of the children of God. What we were, he became, and what he is, we can now become.

We can still agree with Christian tradition by proclaiming that Jesus was the first human being who ascended into heaven, or at the very least, insist that his ascension was somehow eschatologically momentous. This is consistent with the way that Christian tradition reserves the exaltation to God's "right hand" for Jesus alone. Even so, consider for a moment whether this is the main aspect of his after-death experience that differs substantially from what every human being experiences upon dying. In other words, although Jesus' exaltation to God's "right hand" was due in part to his exemplary devotion and obedience (in his human nature), many of the other features of his experience after death were actually quite ordinary. If this is true, then we could be partially justified in looking for models for what happened to Jesus after being crucified among the "normal" (that is, paranormal) happenings that befall humans when they experience death,

---

25. It is very important to understand that to safeguard against undue *spiritual* influences, a believer's intentions must be pure, and especially that the "eye" of intention be cleansed. As Thomas à Kempis memorably put it, students should never travel so far to visit Martha and Mary at Bethany and be more interested in seeing Lazarus than in seeing Jesus. In short, proceed with caution. Unconfessed sins can hamper investigation with a serious danger of leaving the study in a worse state than that in which they started. See Thomas à Kempis, *The Imitation of Christ* (Peabody, MA: Hendrickson, 2004), 95; Matt 12.43–45; 2 Pet 2.18–22.

Postscript

even while restricting the *redemptive* aspect of human life, death, and resurrection to Jesus alone.[26] I anticipate that, with the advancement of our technologies, increasing our understanding of death, it will prove useful for evangelical students to pursue this line of questioning more seriously in the future.

---

26. Still, there is a very real way in which believers help Jesus save the world. Compare the surprising statement in Col 1:24 where the author explains how his own suffering is "completing what is lacking in Christ's afflictions for the sake of his body, that is, the church."

www.ingramcontent.com/pod-product-compliance
Lightning Source LLC
Chambersburg PA
CBHW071709180426

43192CB00051B/1743